MEET MR. GOSPEL MUSIC:

He won the DOVE award for top male gospel singer five years in a row.

He's been given four GRAMMY awards for the best gospel recording of the year.

He's recorded over 75 record albums on the RCA label.

In 1974, he was elected to the Gospel Music Hall of Fame.

His name is James Blackwood, and he's someone you really ought to know.

You can get to know him in this book.

the James Blackwood Story

by
James Blackwood
with Dan Martin

Whitaker House

504 LAUREL DRIVE, MONROEVILLE, PA 15146

504 LAUREL DRIVE, MONROEVILLE, PA 15146

Contents

Foreword by David Wilkerson

I have known James Blackwood for a number of years. He has been a faithful supporter of our ministry as well as many others. More important, I have witnessed the great joy of the Lord in his life and singing. And even though he has lived an animated life, it has not always been easy. That is why I am glad he has finally succumbed to the pressure of his friends and allowed his life story to be told.

The James Blackwood Story is folksy, readable, down to earth, and interesting. It is so good to read an inspiring story in a time when so many sad tales are being told.

If you enjoy the Blackwood Brothers and believe in their ministry, this is the book you must read. And even if you are not addicted to quartet music as I am, you need to read this story to find out why this quartet has stayed on top so consistently over the years.

Introduction

The four voices soar and blend. A beautifully mellow chord comes from the large loudspeakers on the small stage.

The song is about Jesus and His sufficiency.

The muted voices separate, then join again. The tenor is incredibly high, yet sweet. The bass is low, but deep and burnished. The mid-range tones—lead and baritone—are subtle and harmonious.

Each man is singing his note, true and clear and full.

The piano and bass guitar weave their own throbbing undercurrent of melody and harmony, embellishing the hymn of praise.

The Blackwood Brothers Quartet is performing, if performing is the right word to use. It is a combination which meshes a joyous worship service, fulfilling entertainment, and a deeply moving, private prayer time.

As they sing, the power of the Holy Spirit swells and soars like a dove across the congregation. For a while, the building isn't a field house, converted for a moment into an auditorium. It is instead a tabernacle—the residence of God. And God is present, ministering in His Spirit, touching hearts and minds and lives.

The singing undulates, rising and falling in intensity and volume. The singers sing with a fervor which shows a personal acquaintance with Jesus. Their eyes shine, their hands and bodies make gestures, and their voices rise in praise. Their effort is to tell of their Savior.

A concert by the Blackwood Brothers is a shared joy.

But while the audience responds to the quartet, the atmosphere changes as James Blackwood comes on stage.

Across the years, the personnel of the quartet has changed many times. Members have died, been killed, retired, or gone on to other things. But James Blackwood has been with the group since it began more than forty years ago.

The quartet now is a reflection of Blackwood. His personality. His priorities. His principles. His methods and beliefs.

There is a responsiveness between Blackwood and the audience: a kinship, a brotherhood. There is a time of shared laughter—at a joke or a funny bit of patter on stage. There is a time of shared sorrow—remembering parting with those who have died and gone on. There is an assurance—of God and His power. There is a joy —rejoicing in the familyship of brothers and sisters, and looking forward to the blessed hope of Jesus' coming again. There is a peace—knowing heaven is waiting for those who believe in Christ.

Blackwood sings the songs with the touch of reality of one who believes them implicitly. There is faith and assurance in his songs.

The audience senses the care, study and effort Blackwood and the Quartet put into what they are doing. It isn't something slapdash, second-rate. It is not unplanned, nor unprepared. Neither is it so slickly professional that it manipulates the audience with tricks and gimmicks. They are not unmindful of God's leading, the subtle touch of God's power on them and their performance.

The beat picks up. The pace and tempo of the performance changes to that of an evangelistic service: an old-time camp meeting.

"I'll Meet You in the Morning," Blackwood sings. It's an old Albert Brumley song; one of the first songs the original Blackwood Brothers sang back in the 1930s, when poverty and the depression were the common experience, especially in Mississippi.

As Blackwood sings, he jumps off the stage and goes into the audience, shaking hands and greeting folks.

The last stanza ends. The audience lags just a heartbeat before breaking into cheering applause. The lag comes when people are caught up in visions of heaven. They need a few seconds to return to reality. There has been a mental catching up as Blackwood sang.

Blackwood climbs up on a folding chair. "Some people call what we are doing a performance—a show," he says. "But it's not that. We're having a camp meeting here tonight!"

The people cheer.

Blackwood sings another stanza.

He stops. "This song is really my testimony," he says. "Because of Jesus, I know I'll meet you in the morning, over there in heaven. I know I'll meet my folks, my loved ones. I hope all of you here tonight are able to say that.

"I look forward to seeing you over there. But I know I'll meet Jesus there," he adds.

After the audience quiets down, Blackwood calls

11

intermission. People mill around. If there is a superstar of Gospel music—repeated Grammy and Dove awards, top accolades in the Gospel music field—it is James Blackwood. Yet he circulates, touching the people with none of the aloofness which characterizes some superstars. He keeps in contact. A nod here. A smile there. A laugh. A handshake.

The second half of the performance is the same blending of entertainment: the music with its close harmonies, high tenor, low bass and frilly piano; the worship with its praise, evangelism, and joy.

At times the five men on stage—the quartet and James—sing in hushed tones, prayerfully. At times they are exultant, boisterous, militant, driving, convicting. It moves from deeply spiritual moments to hilarity and hoke.

Some songs are slow. Often, though, they sing handclappers and footstompers. All, however, are about God, His Son, His Spirit, heaven, His soon-coming Return, salvation, sufficiency, grace, love.

As God orchestrates a performance—or camp meeting—the mood is infectious. You cannot help responding to it.

At times in the concert, people wipe tears from their eyes. Many heads bow now and again.

A Blackwood Brothers Quartet appearance is as indefinable as a worship service. And it is a worship service. It ends with a song which has an evangelistic appeal, a song about someone who waited too long to accept Christ. It was then too late.

"I hope that song does not apply to anyone here tonight—it need not. 'For God so loved the world, that he gave his only begotten Son, that whosoever believeth in him should not perish, but have everlasting life,' " Blackwood urges, intensity tightening his voice.

He invites the audience—which has somehow become a congregation—to bow their heads, close their eyes and "humble your hearts before God."

"This is the most important part of the night," he says, inviting his listeners to "look into your hearts and see if there is anything there unpleasing to God."

He appeals to people to accept salvation: "to be born again by letting Jesus come into your lives"; and to let the Holy Spirit "show you how to be victorious, overcoming Christians."

People who want prayer are invited to raise their hands. All across the field house/tabernacle hands pop into the air. Blackwood acknowledges them.

"Raising your hand is the first step toward God. He'll make two toward you," Blackwood says.

He offers to pray personally with those who want additional counseling. It's not a gesture. It's for real.

The appearance ends with a prayer. After he has asked God's blessing and has ministered to those who are present, Blackwood waits at the front to pray with those who want to come. A score or more respond, queuing up across the basketball lines on the polished hardwood floor.

Many of the problems they talk about—sickness, tragedy, poverty, tiredness, struggle, discouragement, trial and uncertainty—are problems Blackwood has faced in his own experience.

Other folks talk about joy and peace, happiness and satisfaction. They thank him. Blackwood knows those emotions, too.

Blackwood talks to each person, meeting with them on a one-to-one basis, following Christ's pattern. He shares his assurance and his faith. He shares his joy and his sorrow.

But most of all, James Blackwood—Mr. Gospel Music—shares himself.

Chapter

1

"Palms of Victory
Crowns of Glory,
Palms of Victory
I Shall Wear."

I can hear the words of that old hymn now: slow and reverent, but with a strong message and melody.

My Grandfather Blackwood was singing the song. It was one he sang often. His voice quavered with age and emotion as he sang of heaven and the rewards waiting for those who believe in Jesus Christ.

Grandfather was an elderly man when I was born on August 4, 1919, in Choctaw County, Mississippi, but he was a profound influence on my young life. He died when I was twelve.

He was an old-time singing school teacher and led the music at many a Methodist protracted meeting in our section of Mississippi. Among my earliest memories are of my grandfather singing that old song about heaven.

Sometimes I think God has picked some families for special things.

I know it seems that way with my family, the Black-

15

woods. Grandfather was quite a singer and teacher. My mother and father both sang, but as I look back, neither probably sang very well. My father was a pretty good musician who played the violin in the string band made up mostly of his kinspeople. I have a picture of him made when he was a young man, posing with the string band.

Music has always been a big part of my life. I can hardly remember a time when it wasn't important to us.

Music and prayer were important parts of life, even if money and ease weren't. Maybe poverty and hard work are the reasons we leaned so heavily on God, to talk to Him in prayer and to praise Him in song.

I was born on a farm five miles south of Ackerman, Mississippi, when my folks were already middle-aged; Papa was forty-two and Mama was forty-four.

They already had a grown family. My brother Roy was nineteen. My sister Lena was sixteen, and brother Doyle was eight. Soon after I was born, Roy married and left home. Mama and Papa became grandparents when I was only two years old.

Papa was a sharecropper. He worked hard, striving to wrestle a living from the Mississippi clay. We moved every two or three years, but generally stayed around Ackerman.

Being a sharecropper means you have to share whatever crops you raise with whoever owns the land. The owner lets the farmer use the land for a share of the proceeds.

We were very poor, but God always provided for us. There is a difference between poverty and deprivation. We didn't have much in a material way, but we had each other, food to eat, a place to live, and the power and presence of God in our lives.

He can make a shack into a mansion.

When I was a boy, we raised nearly everything we ate, selling our "money" crop to buy flour, salt, sugar, and coffee. I don't ever remember going hungry, but sometimes the menus were a little monotonous.

Summers were good times for us, growing up. There was a lot of work, but we tried to make even the hard jobs seem like fun.

Corn was something we raised a lot of. In the summer, we had plenty of corn on the cob, but we took a lot of the crop to the grist mill to have it ground into meal. In the winter we ate that corn in cornbread.

We raised peanuts and vegetables, but the real treats were the things which grew wild: blackberries, dewberries, mulberries, nuts, and wild plums. We used everything we could find.

We feasted on fresh blackberry pie and plum cobbler, and Mama put a lot of it up. She canned blackberries and made blackberry jam and jelly. We dried the wild peaches, plums, and apples on top of the house and enjoyed the sweets during the cold winters.

All the meat we ate was raised right on our farm. We had hogs, chickens, and cows; so we always had meat, eggs, butter, and milk. When we killed hogs, we used everything but the squeal, as the old saying goes.

We had food, love, and the presence of God in our home.

Papa believed in hard work, and since cotton was the only cash crop we had, we worked hard. It was hard planting it, hard working it, hard picking it.

We had a planter to help in the first step, but it planted the seeds in a steady stream; so in a couple of weeks we had to thin out the seedlings with a hoe. That job took many hot, tiring hours and I hated it, but I worked, as did the rest of my family.

To keep it from being so bad, I did a lot of singing. Come to think of it, much of my early training and practice was walking in a dry, hot cotton field in Mississippi, swinging a hoe and singing. I sang "Wear A Cheerful Smile" a lot in those days. That was hard, too; wearing the cheerful smile, I mean.

Picking what we planted was hard work, too. We picked the cotton crops in the early fall, and anybody who has ever walked down the long rows pulling the heavy sack knows that's not much fun.

We picked the cotton; we didn't pull bolls. When you pick cotton, you pull the fiber out of the hard hull. When you pull bolls, you pull the whole flower off the cotton plant, hull and all.

The only part of picking cotton that was any fun was riding in the cotton wagon to the gin, ten miles away. We picked the sacks full—usually about a hundred pounds each. When we got fifteen sacks full, we loaded it onto Papa's wagon. The cotton was fluffy and filled the bed of the wagon, which had twelve-foot tall sideboards.

I got to ride all the way to the gin on top of that soft, dirty-white cotton.

But nice as the ride was, the real highlight was when we got to town. We had some money to spend. The cotton ginned out into five hundred pounds of fiber and a thousand pounds of seed. We got paid for the cotton and the seeds.

After it was ginned and we got our money, we went shopping. I got my annual pair of shoes and everybody in the family got their clothing. We laid in our supply of groceries for the winter.

Many days of hard work went into those stiff, new, store-bought shoes and clothes. But they sure did feel nice, knowing we had bought them with money we had earned.

It wasn't all hard work in those days. There was a lot of simple fun, too. We didn't have to have a lot of things to make us happy.

We fished, hunted, and ran in the fields, enjoying the world God had made for us to use.

Poverty made its mark, though, especially at Christmas time. We learned then what it meant to be poor.

One year when I was about seven, I prayed a lot for a little red wagon. I imagined what it would look like. Bright red sides. Rubber wheels. A beautiful thing.

When Christmas Day arrived, I dashed into the front room of our little house. There was a bag of hard candy, a little sack of oranges and apples, and two wrapped packages.

No wagon.

One package had a shirt and the other a pair of overalls. No wagon.

We had Christmas dinner with an uncle who lived over in Louisville, Mississippi. He was rich, in comparison with us. He worked as a baker and had cash money.

When we got to his house, there, under the tree, were two bicycles, a tricycle, two sleds, and a set of trains you wound up with a key. There were toys and games and wonderful things.

19

And a wagon. It was red and beautiful, the most beautiful thing you can imagine.

My heart fell. I wanted a little red wagon all my own. So bad I didn't know what to do. There was no wagon at my house. The wagon that was under his tree was surrounded by so many other good things it wasn't as important to them as it would have been to me. I was envious of them.

It wasn't a very good Christmas for me. And I guess it wasn't very good for my folks, who had tried as hard as they knew how, but still couldn't afford the things they wanted to give their children.

They didn't talk much as we went back home.

As the months passed, so did my conscious desire for a wagon.

But one spring morning—after the robins had returned to Mississippi, and the leaves were peeping out of the buds—Mama woke me up.

"James," she called. "James. Get up or you'll miss the school bus."

I rolled out of bed. Not because I wanted to, but because I had to. I stumbled into the front room. I rubbed my eyes to get the sleep out of them. And there it was! A wagon! Bright red! I couldn't believe my eyes.

"It looks like Santa Claus finally got around to us," Mama said, a smile playing around her lips.

I still couldn't believe it. I couldn't take my eyes off the bright red wagon. It was just like I had dreamed it would be. It had bright red sides and rubber wheels.

Mama finally got me on the bus for school, but I couldn't think about schoolwork that day. All I could think about was my shiny red wagon.

Santa Claus hadn't forgotten me after all.

When school was out, I could hardly wait for that bus to let us off at home. I finally coaxed Doyle into taking me for a ride in the shiny wagon. I kept talking about Santa Claus.

"James," Doyle said, "do you really believe that Santa Claus stuff?"

Doyle was fifteen. He was a man of experience. But here he was expressing doubt about Santa Claus.

I defended Santa Claus: "Mama said there is a Santa Claus. She said he would bring me a wagon.

"And," I gestured at the shiny red wagon, "he did."

Doyle didn't say anything. He just looked at the ground.

I was uncertain. "Isn't that right, Doyle?"

I was really getting confused about our conversation.

Doyle looked confused himself. Finally he blurted: "Listen, James. Mama has been saving her egg money ever since Christmas Day just to buy this wagon for you. I saw the postman bring it day before yesterday."

We looked at each other.

Then Doyle said: "Hop in. I'm going to give you a real fast ride back home. Hold on."

When we got home, I jumped out and ran inside.

Mama greeted me. "How do you like the new wagon Santa Claus brought you?"

"Oh, Mama," I began. "It's—it's—it's such a wonderful wagon." Then, I ran to my Mama and threw my arms around her and hugged her as hard as I could.

I could feel her stroking my hair. Then, she gently pushed me back. She bent down and kissed my cheek.

When I looked at her, Mama was crying.

21

I guess I'll never know the sacrifices Mama and Papa made for us, back there in the good old days of poverty, hard work, love, and faith.

Chapter
2

"For God so loved the world that he gave his only begotten Son that whosoever believeth in him should not perish, but have everlasting life."

Papa was reading. His head was bent over the Word, streaks of silver showing in his dark hair in the soft kerosene lantern light.

He held the big old Bible softly, easily, and lovingly in his work-hardened hands. They were rough. The fingernails had split. Calluses made his hands stiff. But they were gentle hands, for all their roughness.

As he read, we sat in a circle in the sparsely-furnished front room of our sharecropper house. Mama. Papa. Doyle. Me. Listening as Papa sounded out the words about Jesus and what He does for us.

Every day we read from God's Word and prayed. Sometimes we would sing a hymn. Often we didn't.

It was in these moments that our strength was renewed, that our faith was revived, and we entered into that rest that God has provided for people who trust in Him.

I grew up watching Mama and Papa have a real relationship with God. They taught us kids the worth and value of prayer, faith, and love.

Every morning after Mama had gotten through with the breakfast dishes and had made the beds, she would get her Bible and head out the back door.

I often followed her when I was small.

She went to a particular spot beside the painted fence which surrounded our garden. Then she knelt to pray.

"There is a name I love to hear—
I love to sing its worth—
It sounds like music to mine ear—
The sweetest name on earth," Mama sang.

"Oh, how I love Jesus,
Oh, how I love Jesus.
Oh, how I love Jesus,
Because He first loved ME."

Mama always sang a verse of a song as she went out for her prayer. Often it was "Oh, How I love Jesus." But sometimes she sang "Close To Thee," or another old-time hymn.

Then Mama began to pray. I will never forget the sound of her voice as she talked to God there in the cool of the Mississippi morning, kneeling down on the red clay beside the painted picket fence.

I will never forget, nor will I ever get away from, my Mama's prayers.

Mama was brought up a Baptist and Papa was a Methodist, but after they married, they went to the Baptist church.

In the fall of 1918—a year before I was born—a brush arbor meeting was held in Fentress, about a mile and a half from where they were living.

All of the revival meetings—or protracted meetings, as

24

they were called in those days—were held in brush arbors. The arbors were prepared when men went into the woods and cleared an area large enough for about two hundred people.

The trees were cut into posts, which were planted in the ground three to four feet apart. Thinner trees were cut and laid across the tops. Then branches and leaves were interwoven into the sides to keep out the sun.

The "pews" were made with long logs. Planks were put on top of them for seats.

The whole arbor area was lit by kerosene lanterns because sometimes the preachers—like Paul—preached late into the night.

That 1918 revival changed the life of the Blackwood family.

It was an unusual sort of meeting, of a kind that hadn't been held in our part of Mississippi before. There had been protracted meetings, but this was a protracted pentecostal meeting.

A man named Z. D. Simpson was preaching.

Mama and Papa took Lena and Doyle with them to the meetings. Roy already had left home by that time.

Brother Simpson thundered and wooed as he presented the Gospel. He forcefully emphasized that people have to be "born again."

"Unless you're genuinely born again, you'll never get to heaven," he shouted.

"It's not how good you are.

"It's not how many good things you do.

"It's not where you go to church.

"It's only the blood of Jesus that can save you."

Not only did Brother Simpson preach about being born again, he preached about New Testament Christianity, and something new: the Full Gospel.

The Full Gospel he emphasized included salvation, the infilling of the Holy Spirit, and divine healing.

Mama and Papa knew about these things. They'd read about them in the Bible. They knew about the Day of Pentecost and the miracles of healing in the Book of Acts.

"These things didn't just happen to the Apostles," Brother Simpson said. "They are for today. They're for you. They're for me."

Mama knew from the instant Brother Simpson preached about these things that they were for her. When the invitation was given, she was the first one to go forward.

It must have surprised members of the congregation who knew Carrie Blackwood as a good church woman, and as a Christian.

But that night under the brush arbor in Fentress, Mississippi, Mama settled her spiritual questions, once and for all.

"It was just like someone touched me on the shoulder," she told me. "Doyle was asleep on my lap, so I laid him down on the seat, and started forward."

Mama came back to her seat after praying with Brother Simpson. She was overflowing with praise and joy. She raised her hands to the Lord and told people how God had blessed her that night.

A few nights later—during the same revival—Mama received the infilling of the Holy Spirit. The change it made on her life has radiated and spread as it has touched the lives of all the Blackwoods.

Even me, and I wasn't born yet.

Mama was the first to be filled with the Spirit, but since her experience that crisp fall night under the woven tree branches in that old brush arbor, she has prayed God's blessings and the Spirit's filling down on the Blackwood family.

I am convinced it is her prayers which have carried us through our times of trial and tribulation, and have kept us going during the years we have been singing.

Mama had a heavy burden for all the Blackwoods. She began to pray for each one: name by name, place by place, person by person, need by need. Every day, she went out under a large old oak tree, just out of sight of the house. There she talked to God about her kinspeople. She also talked to God about them as she knelt by the old picket fence.

Soon, she had prayed and fasted her family and many of Papa's people into salvation and the infilling of the Spirit. Not all the Blackwoods went along with this new experience. But Roy is an example of how God answered Mama's prayers.

Many days Mama stood out under that old oak tree and prayed about her eldest son. She lifted him up and claimed him for God.

Roy was working away from home as Mama was praying for him. One night he went up to his room after he got off work. As he looked out the window, he suddenly began to weep. He didn't know why. It was unusual for him.

Soon, he quit his job and came back home.

"I knew Mama and Papa had accepted Christ into their hearts, fully and completely, at the meeting in Fentress,"

Roy said. "I knew they had changed, and were conse-crated in their lives and their church work.

"As for me, I suddenly awakened to the love and oppor-tunities for service that were available to those who would follow in His footsteps," Roy added.

Roy was saved shortly after he came home. God soon called him into the ministry and he was filled with the Holy Spirit.

It was into this Spirit-filled, miracle-believing family that I was born.

As a result of the Fentress revival, the Mount Olive Church of God was founded. Papa and Mama were char-ter members of the little church which was about a mile down the road from our house.

A series of meetings was held in the church in the summer of 1923, when I was four years old. In those days, revival meetings were held twice a day—morning and evening.

After the service one hot summer Tuesday, some neighbors came over to our house for lunch. Just after the meal was finished, the folks went out on the front porch to sit and rest.

Someone spotted smoke over in the direction of the church, and everybody rushed over back to the church as fast as possible. By the time they arrived, the church was a pile of smoldering ashes.

For the rest of the meeting—and the rest of the summer—the services were held in brush arbors.

The men, including Papa, went to work to rebuild the church. Erection of a church is a labor of love. For many Christians, the church is as dear to them as their own home, or even more so. The men did the actual building, fitting the beams and walls together, and the women had the task of keeping things cleaned up as the work went on.

When the new church was finished, Mama took me up there to help clean it up before the first meeting. She used an old sage broom to sweep it up.

I've been in a lot of fine churches since those days, but that little old building was the finest thing I ever saw. I remember the way the floors looked, and the walls. I can still hear the wheezy old pump organ.

We'd gather around that organ and sing all the old, wonderful songs. "Rock of Ages." "The Old Rugged Cross." "Pentecostal Power." "Fairest Lord Jesus."

The old building was lit by kerosene lanterns. An old potbellied stove was our central heating system. It was in the center of the room and we all huddled around it in the winter time, burning up on one side and freezing on the other.

I remember this old church best, because it was in it that I came to know Jesus as my own, personal Savior.

It was in the summer of 1925, when I was six years old. A revival was going on. The church was packed and the windows were all open because people who couldn't get in stood around outside and listened to the preaching and singing.

I couldn't sit still during the meetings. The Lord was talking to me about Jesus and about being born again. Finally, on the third night of the meeting, I went down to the old altar at the front.

I confessed my sins and asked Jesus to save me and come to live in my heart. He did, just like He promises in His Word. It was a wonderful experience for me.

Even now, I remember what it was like that night years

ago, in rural Mississippi, when I became a part of the family of God, and was born again. I have enjoyed the fellowship of my Savior—the One who is closer than a brother—since that day.

The members of that little church also exercised a strong faith which may be responsible for my being here at all.

A couple of years after I was saved, I got scarlet fever. The childhood disease was worse in the days before antibiotics and miracle drugs than it is now. Many lives were claimed by it.

Mama thought I had recovered after a few days, and let me walk with her to a neighbor's home, about two miles away. I got there okay, but on the way back, I started to feel real bad.

I was having a relapse. My body began to swell. My wrists expanded until it looked like the skin would burst. Mama and Papa thought I was going to die.

Papa sent word to town for a friend to telephone Roy, who was a minister in North Carolina, and Lena, who lived in Chattanooga. Papa told his friend to tell Roy and Lena to hurry home because I was so ill.

The news was hard on them.

They were both much older than I. Lena had been my baby-sitter for the first two years of my life. She took care of me, almost being a second mother to me, until she married and moved away. Roy was old enough to be my father. In fact, his son, R. W., was only two years younger than I was.

Both Lena and Roy started as soon as they got the message, expecting to get there for my funeral.

They all figured without the power of God, though, and

the faith of a few church members.

Several families from the church had been praying for me, but on the day after I became so seriously ill, they came to our house to pray.

I remember lying in bed and looking out the screen door. It was in the summertime, and I watched as they drove up in buggies and wagons.

They filed in and stood around my bed. Many of them were crying. They knelt down and began to pray for me.

One of the men was kneeling at the head of my bed. He reached out and touched me on my feverish forehead.

"Lord, we know You made this child," he prayed. "We know You have something for him to do. I know You have said in Your Word that we are healed by Jesus' stripes. Lord, I claim healing for James, in the name of Jesus."

The instant his hand touched my head, I knew I was healed.

The swelling started to go down. The people stood around my bed and watched my body return to normal.

There was no way to contact Roy and Lena. They came expecting to find me dead, but by the time they got there, I was out in the fields working.

This dramatic demonstration of the power of God, combined with the simple faith and prayer life of my parents, has had a dramatic influence in my own life and career.

Chapter
3

The long hickory pointer tap danced across the blackboard.

"What's that, James?" Mr. Ray asked.

It was one of life's longest moments as I stood there in Clear Springs Baptist Church that warm summer night.

I knew the diamond shape was "mi." I had a hard time singing it, though.

Finally, I sang: "Mi."

"That's right, James," Mr. Ray said.

The pointer darted to another shape. This time it was a triangle.

"Do," I sang, a little easier.

In the thirties, the country singing schools taught the shape note style of singing. Each shape represented a note on the musical scale.

Vardaman Ray took me through the whole scale and back again, pointing at egg shapes, teardrops, rectangles, diamonds, and half circles.

He had been drilling us on how to sing correctly, and how to sight read quickly.

I think he must have known I was holding hands with

my new girlfriend on the back row. Holding hands under the songbook was an added plus in any singing school.

When the singing school at Clear Springs Baptist Church had been announced, Doyle and I were excited. We both wanted to go very badly.

Doyle and I had been singing around our section of Mississippi for about three years. We had even won a couple of contests with our singing, but we wanted to go to a singing school to learn how to sing correctly.

We wanted to go. Mama and Papa encouraged us to go. But it was during the depression and money was tight. We had food and a house, but very little money.

Mama and Papa talked about what they could do to raise the necessary six dollars to send their sons to the ten-day singing school.

Finally, Mama sold some chickens to raise the necessary cash.

I often wonder where we would be if it hadn't been for those chickens of Mama's.

Doyle and I worked in the fields all day and then rode our old plow horse over to the church, some three miles from our home, for the two-hour sessions each night.

The first thing we learned was how to distinguish a pitch: how to recognize a note when we saw it written on paper. We learned how to sound that pitch correctly.

That's what I was doing standing in front of the school singing. Mr. Ray believed in teaching by drill. He drilled and drilled. Sometimes he would call on people individually, and other times he would have the whole class sing as he pointed that long hickory rod at the blackboard.

Mr. Ray was a well-known singer in our area. He had his own quartet, which made him something of a celebrity. The Ray Brothers Singers sang around the area and had even made a couple of records.

Mr. Ray was a representative of Hartford Music Co. of Hartford, Arkansas. He sold the music they published as well as teaching people how to use it.

Hartford was one of the first of the Gospel music publishing companies. It was founded by E. M. Bartlett—who wrote "Victory In Jesus"—and Albert E. Brumley, who wrote many, many famous Gospel songs. Songs like "Jesus Hold My Hand," and "I'll Fly Away," and "I'll Meet You In The Morning."

I suppose when the school started, I wasn't all that serious about it, but I was serious enough to work all day in the fields and then ride the horse to school at night for ten days.

I was a little nervous and apprehensive at first, but after a while, I got right in the swing of it, because most of the people who were there were home folks.

We got a foundation of music which has served us well across the years. A beginning knowledge of reading music, theory, harmony, and basic things like that.

When I was about eight, Doyle and I started singing duets. We couldn't read the music, so we just memorized the tune and words. Doyle had a little round "tater bug" mandolin which he used to accompany us.

His voice had changed, so he sang baritone lead. I sang the harmony. My voice hadn't changed yet, so I sang alto.

We sang at church, at home, at school, at all-day singings. Anywhere anybody would let us, we sang.

An all-day singing was an event in the lives of the people of the rural South. It combined recreation, fellowship, inspiration, and entertainment. After the Sunday morning service, the ladies would spread food on a long table under the shade trees near the church.

People were poor, but fried chicken, home grown vegetables, home-baked bread, pies, and cakes were there in abundance. People got to eat their fill and then spend the afternoon singing about how good God is.

Doyle and I attended these all over the county and were always asked to sing.

We sang about heaven, about death, about prayer, about living.

One song we sang a lot was about death. The theme was that no matter how wealthy a person is, when he dies, six feet of earth makes everybody the same size.

We still occasionally sing one of the songs we sang then. It's called "Don't Be Knocking." It's different and gets lots of response.

The theme is that if you see your brother failing in the things he tries to do, "Don't be knock, knock, knocking him around. Do your best each day to help him and he will do as much for you."

We put on a little show for the people. Toward the end of the song I would say: "Don't be knocking, kicking, and punching him around," and I would punch, knock, and kick Doyle. Everybody but Doyle liked that.

Sometimes I look back and think about how the Lord provided for us in those hard times. Communities were closer-knit and people made their own entertainment in those days.

People would get up contests in schools around the area. Merchants donated goods for prizes. A sack of flour, a can of shortening, a pair of overalls, a shirt, a sack of sugar.

Right after Doyle and I started singing, we entered a contest at Union School, which was near home. We sang a duet.

Doyle and I won first prize. We took home a whole back seat full of groceries.

After that, we entered every contest we could find. We needed the prizes.

Singing also provided other needs. Like clothing.

My Uncle Remer was a railroad engineer who lived in Jackson, Tennessee. He came down to visit us and told us there was going to be a big all-day singing in Jackson the next Sunday. Doyle and I wanted to go with him, but I had a problem because I didn't have clothes good enough to attend a singing in a place like Jackson.

"All I've got is hand-me-down clothes," I told him. "They're not good enough to wear up there."

"Don't you worry about that," he told me. "I'll get you some clothes."

So, we went home with Uncle Remer and the next day he took me to downtown Jackson and bought me a new outfit. It was the first time in my life I had ever had a dress coat to wear that was not secondhand.

I sure was proud of it.

On Sunday, Uncle Remer took us to the big singing. When it came our turn to sing, they had to put me up in a chair so I'd be tall enough for the people to see me.

We were the hit of the singing.

When it was over, the promoters took Doyle and me down to the radio station. We sang that Sunday afternoon on the radio. It was the first time we ever proclaimed Christ over the air.

But back to Mr. Ray's singing school.

Before the ten-day session was over, he asked Doyle and me if we would like to sing in a new quartet he was forming. He must have heard something in our singing, undeveloped as we were.

We were thrilled. A singer from Ackerman—Gene Catledge—would sing bass; Mr. Ray would sing lead; Doyle would sing baritone. I—still with an unchanged voice—sang tenor. Except that I sang it in an alto voice.

Right after the singing school, our new group was asked to sing at Concord Baptist Church, just south of Ackerman.

It was our first performance as a quartet.

We met that Sunday morning for the services—it was an all-day singing with dinner on the grounds. After dinner, we went out under the shade trees and rehearsed a couple of songs from a new Stamps-Baxter Convention Song Book.

Mr. Ray insisted on singing things right. He wanted the parts to be just so. Sometimes we went over the songs time and again.

It was time. We were due to take our part in the singing.

Mr. Ray's new quartet headed toward the door.

We were going into the church to sing together in public for the first time. It was a heady experience for me.

But Mr. Ray's quartet didn't have a name.

As we got to the door, somebody—I don't remember who—suggested a name and we became the Choctaw County Jubilee Singers.

Well, it was Choctaw County, Mississippi. We were singers and we had to have a name.

We sang together about a year before disbanding. But it was the start of a career that has led me hundreds of thousands of miles around the world, and into the lives of millions of people, many of whom have accepted Christ as their Savior through the ministry of music of The Blackwood Brothers Quartet.

Chapter
4

"Lord, You've got to help me."

That was me. Praying.

I was in a mess. There I was, standing before all those people—well, twenty-five people at least.

I didn't have anything else to say. I'd taught everything I knew. I wished I'd never let Doyle talk me into taking his place teaching the singing school at Batesville.

It all started simply enough.

After we attended Mr. Ray's singing school and sang with his quartet for a while, Doyle started teaching singing schools around the country. I went with him as his "demonstrator."

When I was about fourteen, Doyle asked me if I would teach one of the schools for him.

"James, there is a church up near Batesville. They want a singing school. They called me and wanted me to come up but I can't go. Why don't you teach it for me?"

I was dumbfounded. I wanted to go. But I also didn't want to go.

"I've never taught one before," I stammered.

"Well, you've been to a lot of them. You've seen me teach them, and you've seen brother Roy teach them. You ought to know how to teach one as well as anyone."

I thought about it. I prayed about it. Finally, after the people at Batesville insisted they would like to have me come and teach the school, I agreed.

I got up there, and everything started just fine. I taught the shape notes, the theory, how to recognize a pitch, how to harmonize.

The only thing was that I taught everything I knew in three nights. The school ran ten nights. It was a mess.

"Lord, You've got to help me. I'm in a mess," I prayed as I stood there.

He gave me the answer, as He has given the answer to many prayers since. I started over and taught all the lessons again. Shape notes, theory, pitch recognition, harmony. I drilled and drilled.

I reviewed.

We sang a whole lot. I hoped the people wouldn't notice we were singing a lot and I wasn't teaching much.

At the end of one of those singing schools, it was the custom to have a program on the last night. I couldn't get many of the people to participate in the program, so it wound up with me doing most of that, too.

When I prayed, I also told the Lord I'd never start another of the singing schools if He would help me through that one.

After it was over, and when I was relating this disaster to Doyle, he tried to reassure me: "We'll go over it, and next time you'll do better."

"There won't be any next time," I told him. God kept His part of the deal. I got through the singing school. I kept my part. I have never conducted another singing school.

42

Prayer got me through that singing school. Prayer also kept us going during the next few years, when we were trying to get started. The going was rough and we had a tough time getting established.

Not long after my disastrous singing school experience, Doyle moved to Birmingham, Alabama to start singing with the Homeland Harmony Quartet.

They had a radio program there every morning, and they sang all over the area. Doyle sang with them for a while, and grew as a singer.

Roy was pastoring churches around the country. Early-day pentecostal ministers were sort of like share-croppers. They lived pretty poor and moved quite a bit.

Roy and his son R. W.—who was only two years younger than me—sang in the churches they pastored. Wherever Roy was preaching, he established a quartet, and they continued to sing.

When Doyle moved away, I sang with every group I could find, trying to stay in the singing business.

In 1934, Roy, R. W., and Doyle all moved back to Ackerman, where we were living. I was fifteen at the time, R. W. was thirteen, Doyle was twenty-three and Roy was thirty-four.

We had talked about the possibility of starting a Black-wood Brothers Quartet with the four of us singing.

We decided to begin. From that small decision in rural Mississippi, the Lord began a worldwide ministry. It seems to me like many wonderful things come from small decisions like that.

Doyle sang bass and played the guitar. We didn't have a piano in those days, and sang unaccompanied. Doyle picked.

Roy sang the lead.

Both R. W. and I were altos. My voice was in the changing stage, but I was still an alto. R. W. was two years younger than I was, and was sure-enough alto.

We couldn't both sing alto, although both of us were familiar with singing that part. R. W. sang alto in his dad's quartets. I sang alto with Doyle when we sang together.

We solved the problem for a while by letting R. W. sing alto. Roy sang the lead and I sang the baritone part, an octave high.

When my voice finished changing, I switched to regular baritone.

Later, when R. W.'s voice changed, he took over the baritone, I went to lead, and Roy sang first tenor.

If we had not had the feeling that God was in our singing, I don't know if we could have continued even then.

We didn't make enough money with singing to live on, giving most of our concerts for free-will offerings. We rehearsed our songs—singing mainly from the Stamps or Hartford books—at home, and would sing anywhere within driving distance.

We had to work on the farm to make a living. So for a year—from 1934 until 1935—we worked day and night.

From the beginning, Roy lectured us about our ministry.

"Now, boys," he said, "we must sing the words of this song clearly. I want the people to hear what we are saying.

"If people can't hear what we are saying, we might just as well be saying 'fe, fi, fo, fum.' I've been preaching for eighteen years. The *message* is the thing.

44

"We are singing so the message of the song can be heard. If people don't hear about how Jesus died for their sins, how will they ever know what He did for them?"

Roy drummed it into our heads that we had to enunciate the words or what we were doing would mean little or nothing.

The emphasis on enunciation has been the thing which has characterized The Blackwood Brothers sound for more than forty years.

We sang everywhere we could get a booking: at churches, schools, all-day sings, revivals.

But it was in the depression. Times were rough. Money was scarce.

We were raised poor, so poverty was nothing new to us. I thank God for the way I was raised. My papa believed in hard work and keeping on when times were bad. My folks—but particularly my mama—were strong in faith.

I remember hearing the Yodeling Blues Singer —Jimmy Rodgers—in the early days. Country music was just getting started good and there was a lot of folk and country music going around.

I liked it, but there was something lacking to it.

I sang that kind of music, but I always came back to singing the Gospel music rather than folk or country. I will always believe that the Christian training I received, the Christian home I grew up in, the family worship I participated in each day, and the regular church attendance had a great part to play in it.

Even when Doyle and I started singing duets together, I think I knew something unique was happening.

When we first started singing together as The Blackwood Brothers Quartet, there was something different about what we were doing. God seemed to have picked us out as a family to give us special talents and He also seemed to be using us to provide special ministry and special blessings through our singing.

I am thankful that we grew up in a time when people got together for community and all-day singings.

In the rural South, there was very little the people could do and few places to go to even if they had the money and the time. Most of the effort of life was spent in just living.

But the people got together for singings. It was a time of fellowship, entertainment, and inspiration. Church was just about the only place there was to go.

The all-day singing came up as a community and family affair. People got together and denominational bounds were transcended. The all-day singings brought together Pentecostals, Methodists, Baptists, Presbyterians, and others.

People enjoyed singing. They liked the tunes, the melodies, and the harmonies of Gospel music. Many of the denominational people even liked the beat.

But the Pentecostals were the first denomination to use our type of Gospel music. They were more given to singing songs with a beat. They weren't afraid to clap their hands and pat their feet.

The denominational people wouldn't use our type of music in their services, but they would generally sing and clap their hands and pat their feet during the all-day singings.

For many years, "Stamps-Baxter" was almost a bad word among the denominational churches. The Baptists and Methodists wouldn't sing their songs because the music had a beat and they felt the message wasn't deep enough.

Some of the criticism was justified, but much of it wasn't.

So God knew what He was doing when He put us in the Church of God, and in the rural South of the 1930s. It was a time when our kind of singing caught hold.

I'm glad for my pentecostal upbringing in another way, too. I grew up in an atmosphere where people expected miracles, and believed in the power of God.

Many is the time I have seen Mama get happy in church and begin to shout. Those were the days of shouting Christians. Mama would get happy and stand in the aisle and shout until her long hair fell down her back.

Mama also experienced a healing as the result of her being filled with the Holy Spirit. For years before that, she had been troubled with a series of chronic ailments, including migraine headaches.

Mama was often unable to work because she was constantly sick in those days before I was born. She had a series of what were then known as "female troubles."

"We didn't know to pray for the sick. We were Christians, but we just didn't know we could pray for healing," Mama told me. "When I was filled with the Holy Spirit at the Fentress meeting in 1918, the Lord took away some of my ailments."

But Mama still had "sick headaches," as we called them. Papa often thought she was dying, she would get so sick.

But Mama told me how God removed the migraine headache problem from her: "The doctors couldn't do anything for me. They tried different kinds of medicine, but none of it worked. The sick headaches had been going on for years.

"A couple of weeks after I was filled with the Spirit, I woke up with another one of those terrific headaches. My stomach was very upset, and I vomited.

"My head felt like it was splitting open.

"I got up and went outside in the backyard. It was still in the summertime and the night was deep, deep blue with millions of stars making little lights in the sky.

"I looked up at the starry heavens that God created. 'Lord,' I said. 'You have healed my soul. Now I ask that You heal my body.'

"I had never been taught about anything like that, but I knew if God could heal my soul, He must be able to do something about those terrible painful headaches."

Mama never had another of the "sick headaches" in her life.

She died when she was eighty-seven, and she told me the story when she was in her eighties. She had never had another headache after God touched her body.

It was in this context—and with this faith—that we began our ministry of music. If God had not been directing my life, and the lives of my brothers and nephew, I don't think we could have weathered what we started. I don't think we would have weathered some of the hardships we went through.

But God kept speaking to us. We saw people blessed when we sang. We saw people saved. God kept telling us He intended for us to be together: to keep on singing, to be determined.

He told us not to separate, but we did once, for nearly two years.

It was in 1935, and times had gotten even worse. Roy had a family. He and his wife, Susie, had had another son: Cecil Stamps Blackwood. Now brother Roy had the responsibilities of a wife and two sons.

He was called to a Church of God in Fort Worth. Because of economic conditions, he accepted the call and moved to Texas.

Of course, R. W., his son, went with him.

That left Doyle and me.

Doyle went back to Birmingham and started singing with the Homeland Harmony Quartet.

I was the lone member of the quartet at home. I was sixteen. I had quit school when we started singing together, and I continued to sing wherever I could—in solos, in duets, and with any quartet we could put together.

But there was something missing. God had intended for us to sing together. All the time we were separated I prayed that God would bring us back together and fulfill the burning desire in my heart.

God had given us a ministry. It was a ministry of singing, entertaining, and witnessing about the Lord Jesus Christ.

What He had started He would bring to conclusion.

Chapter
5

My prayers were answered; we were together again.

It was 1937, and we had been apart for a long time —nearly two years. I prayed a lot in those years, asking God to bring our quartet back together, and to help us get started again.

Roy moved back to Ackerman after pastoring the Fort Worth church. R. W. was with him. By this time my nephew was a handsome young man with a sweet, mellow, baritone voice.

Doyle, too, had come back. He had been singing over in Alabama, but when he heard Roy was back, Doyle came home.

We were a family quartet again. The Blackwood Brothers Quartet was in its second start.

This time, we were going to make a go of it. We had a ministry to perform, and a task to do. We had something to give to the people. We had a long way to go, but we were going to take that first step.

We might have to chop cotton and saw lumber to get enough cash to live on, but we were determined to make a success of it.

We began, as we had the first time, by singing anywhere we were invited. To pay the way, we worked on Papa's farm; but it would barely support him and Mama, much less six more of us.

The four of us got a contract cutting timber to help out with the expenses. Usually, we practiced our songs at home, but while we were out in the woods, we sang as we sawed and chopped. We had a pretty good metronome with the chop-chop-chop of the axes against the Mississippi pine trees. Singing while we sawed took some of the monotony out of the work.

Our quartet had basically the same arrangement as before, except that R. W. and I no longer sang alto. Doyle played the guitar and sang bass; Roy had the high tenor; R. W. sang baritone; and I was the lead.

Most of our sings were for "free will" offerings. There was a lot of "free will" but not much "offering" in those days because the poeple we sang for were as broke as we were.

Sometimes, when we sang in schools or other places, an admission was charged. During hard times, the cost to get in to hear The Blackwood Brothers Quartet sing was a nickle for children and a dime for adults. Most of the time, the proceeds were less than five dollars a night. Expenses only.

For the most part, we were locally known, and we knew that if we were to make a go of singing for a living, we would have to spread our base of operation.

The way God provided was radio. Radio has played a large part in our ministry across the years, and it was the device the Lord used to give us our first big "break."

Not long after Roy, R. W., and Doyle moved back to

Ackerman in 1937, a radio station was put in in Kosciusko—about forty miles from home. It was a little 250-watt operation in an old house. But it was still a radio station.

Then, it probably had a listening area with a radius of about a hundred miles from Kosciusko. Now, a station with power like that is in competition with bigger, more powerful stations. But then it was a God-send. It expanded our view hugely.

Sometimes I think prosperity has ruined our appreciation of what God does for us. Then, we were thrilled that God opened up the little 250-watt station for us.

Now, it seems many people are not satisfied until they have a Hollywood-size epic production, perfect in every detail.

God leads one step at a time, not in huge leaps. At least He leads us that way.

Radio station WHEF was within driving distance. It was unaffiliated with a network and they were always looking for somebody to sing, play a fiddle, pick a guitar, preach, talk, or do something.

Even in those days, the rules made them separate the advertisements with something. Something had to fill the air time between the commercials.

We talked about going to Kosciusko for a while. The station was there. The more we prayed about it, the more it seemed that we should go there and get on radio.

Finally, one Sunday we drove down to see if we could get on the air. It was a big step of faith, but we would lose nothing if the management gave us a negative answer.

We found the old house. We went in and told the man

who met us we had a quartet and would like to get on the radio.

He looked us over. We were anything but impressive. We were a bunch of country boys.

God nudged the man. It was a long moment as he looked at us.

"All right," he finally said. But he wasn't too impressed and gave himself a hedge. "I'll put you on for fifteen minutes."

He wasn't very sure of us. In fact, we weren't very sure of ourselves. Doyle and I had sung on the radio once before, back in Jackson, Tennessee, with my uncle Remer Blackwood.

It was going to take the Lord's power to let us sing and sing well before that microphone in an empty studio. We were used to singing before audiences, and we didn't know what it would be like to sing to a bare room.

When people respond to you, you sing—or preach or pray or teach—better. We weren't at all sure what would happen when we sang there in the studio.

"Lord, give us the power to sing for You," Roy prayed as we went in. "We want to glorify Your Name. Let us bless the people who are listening to us today.

We went into the studio, which was a converted room in the old house.

The man we had talked to was not just the talent scout. He was the whole shooting match. He was the manager, the announcer, the secretary, the engineer, and the switchboard operator.

Soon he pointed to us. We started singing.

Before we were through the first stanza, the phone began to ring. Calls from Kosciusko. Calls from all around

54

the area. Long distance calls—and that was unusual in those poverty-stricken days.

As soon as the manager-announcer-secretary hung up, the phone rang again. He wrote the requests and dedications on slips of paper, handed them to us and we acknowledged them on the air.

The first quarter hour passed. That was all he had agreed to let us sing. We looked at him. The telephone was still ringing off the wall. He motioned for us to keep right on singing. We did.

When the second fifteen minutes was over, the phone was still busy. He motioned for us to sing some more. We sang and sang. Before it was over, we sang an hour and fifteen minutes that morning: five times as much as he had agreed on.

He told us there were about sixty long distance telephone calls during that time.

He was pleased with his "find." He asked if we would like to have a regular program on WHEF. We were dumbfounded. God had answered our prayers even better than we could realize.

We agreed on a thirty-minute program every Sunday morning.

Our radio career was on the way.

There was only one hitch. We were radio performers, but we didn't get paid for our singing—although we could announce our engagements and open dates on the show and make our bookings over the air.

We continued to sing on the radio and to go on personal appearances all across Mississippi.

Many concerts were still of the "free will offering" type, but we did charge admission for some.

The tide change'd a little at a concert at the high school in the little town of Noxapater, Mississippi. We thought we were finally in the big time.

We booked a concert there. Admission was still ten cents for adults and five cents for children.

There in Noxapater, we made twenty-seven dollars at the concert. We were overjoyed.

"Man, if we could just average that a night, we'd be rich," I told Doyle. "That'd be $810 a month, if we sang every night. I can't imagine that much money—wow!"

It was a pipe dream. We didn't even begin to earn that much money every night. Most performances still grossed five and ten dollars a shot, which barely covered expenses.

But the Lord was there, encouraging us as we ministered.

Three weeks later, we were booked into Houlka, Mississippi. It was a small town, but the crowd for our concert was tremendous.

When we counted the receipts, they totaled fifty-five dollars. At a nickle or dime a head, that was some crowd.

"Let's just move up here with these people," Roy said. "Man, if they turn out like this, we'll be on our way."

It was not too long after the fifty-five dollar night that we decided to move on to bigger and better things.

Before the decision was made, we talked about it.

"It's a big step to go into singing full time," Roy reminded us. "It is a big step of faith."

We thought about it. Roy had a wife and a small son—in addition to R. W.—to support. Doyle, R. W., and I were not married, but we had to eat.

We remembered the twenty-seven and the fifty-five

dollar concerts. But we also knew most were barely enough to pay expenses. We also knew it would be hard work.

We prayed about it.

Finally, we made the decision to go to Jackson, Mississippi—the capitol and the largest city in the state—and try for a spot on WJDX radio. It would be a full-time place, but we wouldn't get paid for our services there either. We auditioned for—and got—a daily rather than a weekly radio show.

We were to be able to sing and witness every day. But a problem arose. We were committed to sing Gospel music, and the station wanted us to mix some country songs in.

Although we didn't like it very much, we finally agreed to sing some of the popular country and folk songs. But we knew we were Gospel singers. God had called us to sing Gospel, not country music. After a few programs, we got the station management to put the matter to a straw vote by the listeners.

"Folks," Doyle told the listeners on the next program. "We want to know how you feel about our program. Would you like to hear the Blackwood Brothers in an all-Gospel program?"

The response was tremendous. The vote was overwhelming. We went to an all-Gospel program. We never sang "pop" music again.

When we first moved to Jackson, we lived in two rooms in a rooming house hotel near the radio station. Roy, Susie, and Cecil lived in one room. Doyle, R. W., and I lived in the other.

We had only one automobile—an old 1935 Ford Roy bought when he lived in Fort Worth. It was showing the effects of dirt roads and thousands of miles.

Few people realize the importance of a good appearance in a public performance.

"If we're going to communicate the Gospel by song, we will have to dress in a way that will not draw attention to ourselves," Roy told us. "If we are sloppy in any way, this will draw attention away from the music, and away from the Lord.

"It is extremely important for us to keep up a good appearance," he added.

We spent the princely sum of twelve dollars and fifty cents each for four white linen suits. But they were the only ones we had all alike. Because times were so hard and money was so tight, we had paid a little bit down on the suits and paid them off on credit.

Taking care of the suits was a problem, because we were singing nearly every night. We had to be very careful with them. But even when we were careful, they still got pretty dirty.

We didn't have the money to send them to the laundry and have them professionally done, so each week we bundled them up and mailed them to Mama.

I don't know what we would have done without her.

Mama was past sixty, but she would go down to the spring, dip up the water, get the wash pot to boiling and wash our suits. There was no washing machine at the Blackwood place. Mama had to heat the water in a big old wash pot, and then wash the clothing with an old-fashioned rub board and homemade soap.

When the suits were clean and dry, she would go up to the house and fire up the wood cookstove. Even in the heat of the Mississippi summer she heated up that stove because there was no electricity. She had to use the old flat irons to press the suits. Then she'd mail them back to Jackson so we'd have something to wear to our next concerts.

Two mishaps I remember happened to my suit.

The first one came as an accident. The second was not so accidental.

We had a crude public address system mounted on the 1935 Ford. We drove around town advertising our concerts, and then took the horns off the car, for use as loudspeakers at the concerts.

The system ran off the car battery.

One night we were singing and I had to take the battery out of the car to use in the auditorium. I'd already changed clothes and was ready to go on stage.

I got the battery out without any trouble, but as I carried it, I stumbled.

Slop. All over my coat. The battery acid ate a great big hole in my quartet suit.

I had to be the "different" singer in the quartet for a while until we could get the money to buy a new linen suit.

Another accident wasn't so accidental.

We ate at a hamburger stand across the street from the hotel where we lived. For breakfast, we could get an egg, bacon, toast, jelly, and coffee for fifteen cents.

Hamburgers cost a nickle. We usually ate nickle hamburgers for lunch and supper. I ate so many hamburgers at Jackson that I just plain got sick of seeing them. You could doctor them up with lots of stuff like mustard and catsup, but they were still hamburgers. There were times, though, during those early years that we didn't even have the cash for a hamburger. When we were really broke, even a nickle hamburger looked good.

We all had linen suits again and were getting ready to go out on a sing. I was already dressed and R. W. and I ran across the street to get a hamburger.

While we were there, we got into some kind of argument with a boy who worked there. We saw him every day, but for some reason we got into a fuss. We made him mad, really mad.

He picked up a mustard bottle and squirted mustard all over the front of my white linen coat. R. W. and I chased him all over the café, but he finally got into a back room and locked himself in.

I was a mess for the concert that night, but the manager of the place made the guy have my suit cleaned.

We sang out of Jackson for a year and a half, doing one night stands and a lot of traveling while living in two rooms in the hotel and eating nickle hamburgers.

Our career almost died in Jackson, but God moved to keep us on the road.

The 1935 Ford was worn out. We owed more money on it than it was worth. Things got rougher and rougher. Finally we had to let it go back to the finance company.

We didn't have a car. Because we had let that one go back to the finance company, we couldn't find anybody to finance another one for us.

We were almost ready to go back home and give it up. The bank wouldn't give us money for a car without a cosigner. We asked several people, but nobody would help us out.

Without a car, we couldn't travel; and if we couldn't

travel, we couldn't sing. If we couldn't sing, we couldn't make any money at all. It seemed like our ministry had ended.

I'll never know how it happened, except that the Lord intervened.

On an impulse we asked an engineer at the radio station, "Will you sign the note for us at the bank?"

"Yes," he said. Simple as that.

The Lord must have moved on us to ask him and moved on him to say yes. Without him, our career would have ended right there.

We bought a 1938 Ford and continued singing.

God had again kept the Blackwood Brothers on the road.

God kept moving us upward, too. Station WJDX in Jackson was a 5000-watt station. We had come from a 250-watter to Jackson.

Now, in late 1938, we had the opportunity to audition for a 10,000-watt station in Shreveport: KWKH.

We sang on the Louisiana State Singing Convention program and won the right to sing on the powerful radio station which covered Louisiana, parts of Texas, Mississippi, Arkansas, and Oklahoma. Right after we moved to Shreveport, it upped its power to 50,000 watts.

At KWKH, we had two programs a day, at 6:30 A.M. and at 12:30 P.M.

For some unusual reason, I remember the first song we sang on KWKH. It was an old Albert Brumley song: "They Will Welcome Me Back Home."

While we expanded our range on the radio station, we also expanded the distance we traveled to personal appearances. We were following the same pattern we had established in Kosciusko with announcements of engagements and open dates.

We practically lived in our car. We left the noontime broadcast and headed out for East Texas, Louisiana, West Mississippi, Southern Arkansas, or wherever it was we were going to sing that night. We drove into the early morning hours practically every day.

Shortly after we moved to Shreveport, we went to work for V. O. Stamps, president of the Stamps-Baxter Music Co. of Dallas. He had heard us on KWKH and was impressed with our singing and our following.

V. O. Stamps was the daddy of Gospel quartet music. He pioneered both the publishing and the singing of much of what we know today as distinctive Gospel music.

He started with the James D. Vaughan Music Company in Lawrenceburg, Tennessee. They employed some of the early Gospel singers and writers working around 1910 to 1920.

Later Mr. Stamps and his brother, Frank, came into prominence. V. O. started his own quartet, the Stamps Quartet, and his brother had the Frank Stamps All Stars.

Frank recorded for RCA Victor Records in 1927—the first Gospel group to record on a major label. They recorded the world-famous Stamps song, "Give The World A Smile" which was the theme song for all of the Stamps quartets.

V. O. Stamps moved to Jacksonville, Texas, and started the Stamps Music Co. He took J. R. Baxter in with him and the company became the Stamps-Baxter Music Company, which it still is today.

V. O. Stamps got a big break in radio back in 1936 when

he got on 50,000-watt KRLD in Dallas during the State Fair of Texas. He landed two daily broadcasts on the station because the people liked the Stamps Quartet so well at the Fair.

Mr. Stamps also had a fifteen-minute program on a 50,000-watt radio station in Mexico, just across the Rio Grande River from Del Rio. He sold hundreds of thousands of song books with the program on that station.

He soon began organizing other quartets and putting the Stamps name on quartets. They were on local radio stations around the South and represented the Stamps-Baxter Music Company, selling the song books.

V. O. was a big, wonderful man. He had a strong, aggressive personality and was dedicated to promoting the Gospel through Gospel quartet music. He had a listening audience in the millions by the late thirties, and at least fifteen quartets.

The announcers in Dallas referred to V. O. Stamps as "The Man With a Million Friends." He could have been elected governor of Texas if he had wanted to run, because he was so popular.

When God opened the doors for us to go with his successful organization, we became The Blackwood Brothers-Stamps Quartet.

We were still driving the 1938-model automobile we had bought with God's help in Jackson, but when we joined Mr. Stamps he provided a car, song books, and salaries.

We had lived from hand to mouth, subsisting on nickle hamburgers and cosigned car loans. Now, financial security seemed around the corner.

Although we were not owned by the Stamps organization, we did sign on to be their representatives. In addition to the automobile—and the first one he gave us was a 1939 Mercury—we profited by selling his song books. Each member of the quartet got to keep up to eighteen dollars and fifty cents a week, depending on how many song books we could sell.

We'd never made that kind of money before. That was pretty good money for four country boys from Ackerman, Mississippi, who had been struggling along near starvation.

Mr. Stamps was good to us. In 1940, he traded in our 1939 Mercury and got us a 1940 Mercury, and then gave us a 1941 Oldsmobile.

When we were in Shreveport, Mr. Stamps wanted us to add a fifth member to our group: a pianist. "The piano is the proper instrument to accompany a Gospel quartet," he told us.

Joe Roper joined us as our first pianist. He was from Alabama and stayed with us only three months.

Then, in succession, we had Wallace Milligan, from Savannah, Georgia, and Marion Snider, the pianist from the original Stamps Quartet.

We'd come a long way since being reunited in 1937. We had a job on a 50,000-watt radio station, a good car, and a salary for the first time. We also were affiliated with a famous Gospel quartet organization.

God had a purpose for us. He was, in His way, providing for us.

Chapter

6

She was beautiful.

She was standing near the back of Weathersby Baptist Church that Sunday afternoon. The aisle was crowded, and there were a whole lot of other people there. But I saw her as she stood there. Only her.

"Hello," I said, after I worked my way around near her. I didn't tell her how my heart pounded, or that I hadn't been able to take my eyes off her during the concert that afternoon.

Or that I had tried to catch her eye. Or that I went out the side door of the church and came around to the main door to get close to her.

I didn't know her name, but I did know I was very attracted to her.

She was holding her song book up high. On it was written: "Miriam Grantham."

It rang a bell.

"Miriam Grantham?" I asked. "Miriam Grantham. I remember your name. You wrote us a letter. Didn't you?"

"Yes," she laughed. "I wrote and requested a song."

We talked a little while. I don't know what about. I was busy looking at her.

In a minute, her mother came up. We were going to their home for pie and coffee after the all-day singing.

"Why don't you ride with us?" I asked as we started to leave. "That way you can show us the way to your house."

She agreed and sat next to me. The car was crowded, so she sat close to me.

On the way, she picked up my hand.

"That's a pretty ring you have on," she said. I was glad she held my hand, if even for a little while.

We had pie and coffee, but the main event was when I asked if I could come calling on her.

Her folks agreed and my God-appointed romance began.

When I met Mim, Roy was the only married member of the group. Doyle, R. W., and I were unmarried. Since we had only one car, we took turns "sparking," as dating was called then.

Every night I could, I drove down to see Mim. But soon I wasn't getting the car often enough to suit me. If it wasn't my night, I took the bus.

I just couldn't see enough of Mim.

Her daddy was a mail carrier, and he had weathered the depression pretty well with a steady job and a good income. Mim never knew what it was to want for anything. She didn't know there were people who didn't have enough money to buy anything and everything they wanted to eat.

And I didn't tell her.

When I went to Weathersby to see her, there were some real fringe benefits for a hungry boy like me: her mother almost always loaded down the table with good things to eat. After we were married, she told me her mother couldn't believe how much I could eat. I was short and thin, but I could put away the groceries. They didn't know I had been practically starving for days.

Once when we had an off-day, I rode the bus to Weathersby to be with Mim. The bus ride cost twenty cents one way. I had forty cents, just enough to get there and back.

I was really hungry as I rode the thirty-five miles to Weathersby, looking forward to a good meal at Mrs. Grantham's table. Things had been particularly bad that week.

When I got to their house, Mim met me at the door.

"James, Mama's not feeling well. She has a headache and doesn't feel like cooking. She wants us to go uptown to a restaurant to eat."

I almost fell through the floor.

"What am I going to do now?" I wondered. I had only twenty cents, just enough to get back home. It wasn't even enough to feed both of us even if I hitchhiked back to Jackson.

I was petrified. I prayed for a miracle as we drove to Mendenhall.

When we got there, she pulled into a drive-in.

I had one out. I wouldn't order anything and would just hope her order wouldn't be over twenty cents. Then I'd hitchhike home.

The carhop came over to the car for our order.

"What'll you have?" she said.

"A sandwich and a coke," said Mim.

"I'm not hungry," I said. It was a lie. I was starving to death.

"I really don't care for a thing," I added, unnecessarily.

We chatted until the order came.

"Are you sure you're not hungry, James?" Mim asked several times as we sat there.

"Oh, yes, I'm sure," I said, starving all the time.

The order came. Watching Mim sit there and eat was agony. My mouth watered, but I had to hide it.

The order was within my price range, but when the car hop came back to the car, she went to Mim's side and Mim handed her a bill.

"I'm going to pay for it," I protested.

"Oh, no. Mama gave me money for both of us to eat," Mim said.

It was too late then. I couldn't tell her what had happened. I was too embarrassed.

I didn't tell her about it until after we were married. Years later, it is funny to me, but it is still sad to her.

It sure was hungry riding home to Jackson that night.

While I was dating Mim, Doyle was going with Lavez Hawkins, who was from Forest, Mississippi, but was attending business school in Jackson.

As we all began to get serious, the opportunity to go to Shreveport came along. It was a good move for us professionally, but we sure were far away from our girlfriends.

Doyle was as lonely as I was. Both of us were miserable, and I guess we were both so much in love that we didn't talk about much but getting married. And Lavez and Mim.

We decided to propose.

I did and Mim accepted.

Doyle did and Lavez said yes.

Since we were so far away, we decided to have a double wedding.

The date was set for May 4, 1939. Mim was going to

graduate from high school at the end of April and Lavez would finish business school about the same time.

Doyle and I moved to Shreveport in April. We were making steady money for the first time in our lives. Between us we saved enough money to rent a two-bedroom furnished apartment for thirty-two dollars a month and to make a down payment on two wedding bands.

We also had enough money for gas to drive to Mississippi, get a license to get married, and pay the preacher.

But I was late for my own wedding.

We had it all planned. Doyle and I left Shreveport and thought we had plenty of time. We were behind schedule even before we left, though.

Mim's daddy was getting a little edgy about the delay.

"Mim," he said in a worried voice. "How well do you know this James, anyway?"

He kept watching the clock and saw the hands moving past the appointed time.

We were hurrying, because I knew we were late, too. Our first stop was in Forest for Doyle's bride-to-be. Then we rushed toward Weathersby.

I was two hours late when we finally pulled in.

"See, Daddy. I told you he would be here all right," Mim said. But she looked a little relieved, too.

We headed toward Mendenhall to the county seat to get the licenses. Mim's dad came along with her to speak for her because she was underage.

"How old are you?" the clerk asked her.

"Seventeen," she replied. Mr. Grantham vouched for her to get the license.

The clerk looked at me.

"How old are you?" he inquired.

"Nineteen," I replied.

"Where are your parents?" he asked.

"My parents," I stammered. "Why?"

I'd been out on my own for some years and had been singing with the quartet two years. It didn't dawn on me that I was underage too, since the legal age in Mississippi was 21.

It scared me, though.

"After all this and I still can't get married," I groaned.

The clerk issued us a license, although he knew he wasn't supposed to. But since he knew us, he issued it anyway.

We drove on to Jackson and stood before a Methodist preacher friend of mine and pledged ourselves to each other.

It has been a pledge and a commitment which has gone through the trials and tribulations only a "quartet man's wife" knows.

Mim has put up with a lot, being married to me. It takes a special breed to be married to a quartet man, to be content and not complain.

I am away from home a lot and Mim accepts it. When we are at a concert or convention, she is very understanding and is willing to share my time with other people. Some women might not be content to do that, but Mim has been the perfect wife God intended for me. She has strengthened our ministry and been a source of faith and strength to me.

Mim was a member of the Baptist church when we got married, but she wasn't a Christian. She didn't know it but I did.

She also had the prejudice many denominational people had against pentecostals: she thought everybody who belonged to a pentecostal church got down on the floor and rolled around. Holy Rollers, you know.

I didn't push her. I tried to lead her as gently and as carefully as I could.

And our marriage was really completed during the war, when we were in San Diego.

"You can know it in your head, but unless Jesus is in your heart, you aren't saved," the Free Methodist preacher proclaimed.

"You have to have a personal relationship with Jesus Christ—you have to know He died for your sins—that it was YOU who put Him on that cross," Brother George Gaines told the congregation.

"Head knowledge isn't enough. You have to have heart knowledge too," he said as he stood at the front of the Servicemen's Chapel where we sang during World War II.

As he preached, Mim came to know she was not a Christian. She came to know what spiritual salvation is. She had been a church member, but on that night she became a Christian.

It was something I had been praying for since we married. God answered my prayers.

Mim and I were finally together as children of God.

Chapter
7

"Shenandoah," we chorused. "Where's that?"

Shenandoah was in Iowa but it might as well have been at the North Pole as far as we were concerned. We were southern boys.

It was the spring of 1940. We were getting pretty well known across Louisiana and the surrounding states. Doyle and I had been married a year.

R. W. joined us in matrimony, marrying Elaine Whitehead. All of our singers were now family men.

We were doing pretty well in Shreveport. The station had increased to 50,000 watts. We were singing in personal appearances all over Louisiana and East Texas, Arkansas, and parts of Mississippi.

God was very good to us.

But pick up and move to a foreign country like Iowa?

V. O. Stamps asked us if we would like to move to Shenandoah.

"Boys, my brother Frank has a quartet broadcasting from Des Moines. I need him down here in Dallas. Would you consider going up and swapping places with him?" Mr. Stamps asked.

It was a hard decision for us to make, but Mr. Stamps

had been very good to us. We finally had financial stability. It was necessary for family men.

Eventually, after much prayer, plans were made for us to move to Shenandoah, to take a spot on radio station KMA there.

We left Shreveport in July and moved to Shenandoah. We vacationed on the way, before finally moving in.

Mr. Stamps sent Hilton Griswold—from Cameron, Texas—with us as our pianist.

We knew we were moving out of one phase of our life and into another.

Gospel music was strange to the Midwest. We were strange to the Midwest. All of us—except Hilton—were from central Mississippi. We sounded like it, too.

It was like going to a foreign country. We had never been out of the South before. And there we were in a place where towns and people had strange names.

We had quite a time with pronunciations, particularly with German and Dutch town names.

We heard a lot about it on the radio when we mispronounced a name. The people weren't mad; they just kidded us a lot about it.

In Shenandoah, the radio station we were on—KMA —reached into Iowa, Missouri, Nebraska, Kansas, Minnesota, and South Dakota.

Soon we were on the road continually, traveling hundreds of miles from Shenandoah to sing and then back again each day.

At KMA, we had three daily broadcasts. We were on the air live at 7:30 A.M. and again at 12:30 P.M. We recorded a program each afternoon to be broadcast back at 5:30 A.M. the next morning.

The program was recorded on big acetate or vinyl discs with a cutting needle. There was no editing. We had to do it perfectly or just let it go full of boners.

As we became better known in the Midwest, we traveled every night of the week, usually within a radius of 250 miles, so we could get back in time to sing at 7:30 A.M. the next morning.

It was not uncommon for us to get home at four or five in the morning and drop into bed.

Sleep was precious. I had it perfectly timed: the alarm clock rang at 7:22 A.M. I hopped out of bed, jumped into my clothes, and ran for the car. After a dash to the radio station, I could walk in the door just as Hilton hit the opening notes of our theme song.

God was working as He opened up a big listening audience for us. After we started at Shenandoah, we offered the *Stamps-Baxter News*, a little newspaper published monthly in Dallas.

Mr. Stamps put our picture on the front of the newspaper and told us to offer it free for two weeks. We did, and we had more than 10,000 requests for it.

The station and an advertising agency estimated from the response that we had a million people in our listening audience. After we got established there, we received mail from twenty-seven states and three Canadian provinces.

Also while we were there, we got another plus from Mr. Stamps.

We got a raise to forty dollars a week, apiece. That was big money.

We also had a big new 1941 Oldsmobile to drive, and were associated with a fine organization. For the first time we were making a decent living.

But, even as nice and as big as that Oldsmobile was, I sure did get tired of it after a while.

There is simply no way for five men to ride comfortably for that long in a car.

I tried sleeping sitting up. Then I'd get down on the floor and put my head on the seat. I'd try to lie down. Every position there was, we tried.

There is simply no way to ride comfortably and try to sleep in a car. Not with five full-grown men.

We drove hundreds of miles a week in that big car, taking the chances of highway travel. But God took care of us.

I remember running out of gas during a blizzard—our first blizzard—in November of that year. We were in a remote place in Iowa. It was early in the morning. It was cold. Snow was coming down.

We left Shenandoah with clear weather, en route to northeast Missouri for a sing. On our way back, we ran head-on into the snow storm.

The Blackwood Brothers were Mississippi boys, unused to such things as snow, ice, and freezing rain.

The blizzard hit us, and the car used more gas than we figured it would.

"The car is out of gas," said Doyle, who was driving. He coasted as far as he could and we got out and tried to push for a while.

It was too cold for that. We didn't make any progress. The road was getting slippery. Things got worse and worse. We were freezing.

"You all get back in the car," Doyle told us. "I'll go see if I can find some help."

Doyle walked down the road in the swirling snow as we climbed back into the car. Before long he came to a farmhouse. It was dark. There was no sign of life.

Doyle knocked on the door. There was no answer.

"Hello," he hollered. "Is anybody home? We're out of gas and need some help."

In just a minute a light came on upstairs.

The front door soon opened.

"Are you Doyle Blackwood?" the man asked to Doyle's surprise.

"Yes," said Doyle.

"My wife said it was you. She told me to get up and come down here because she thought she recognized your voice. She listens to you every morning on KMA radio," he told Doyle, who was dumbfounded.

Doyle was our announcer three times a day. His voice became pretty well known throughout the Midwest.

God was looking out for us. It was no coincidence a listener recognized Doyle's voice that night. Or that we got some gas to get us home through our first blizzard.

God kept looking out for us as we traveled the long, lonely highways of the Midwest, crossing the states in good weather and bad, singing about His Son.

Chapter
8

"The Japanese have attacked our naval base at Pearl Harbor."

The worried-sounding voice broke in on our car radio.

"Did you hear that!" I exclaimed.

I reached over and turned up the volume.

"We break into this program to bring you this news bulletin. We repeat. Japanese warplanes have just attacked our naval base at Pearl Harbor in the Hawaiian Islands."

We were stunned.

It was Sunday afternoon, December 7, 1941, a day we shall never forget. The five of us were in our 1941 Oldsmobile, headed for a sing that night.

We couldn't believe our ears. An attack on Pearl Harbor. We knew there was a war going on in Europe and that the Japanese had been preparing for fighting.

But an attack on our base!

We listened to the news reports that afternoon as we drove. What had started as a joyful trip to a concert now became a sorrowful journey. It was a somber performance.

It became apparent how bad the attack had been. Warplanes sank the U.S.S. Arizona, one of our battleships. The army barracks and the airfield had been destroyed. How many casualties there were, nobody knew.

It was the beginning of World War II for the United States.

We continued with our radio broadcasts and concerts for several weeks. We didn't know what the Lord wanted us to do. We didn't know what we should do.

All of us—R. W., Doyle, Hilton, and I—were of draft age. We didn't know how long the war would last or how bad it was going to be. But we knew we probably would be called up for the draft during the next year or so.

Only Roy—who by then was nearly 41 years old —would possibly escape going into the service.

We weren't worried about it. Our nation had been attacked. We were in dangerous times. The possibility of attack on our shores loomed as a very real threat.

But we continued to sing. Sometimes, when you are in a difficult time, facing a difficult decision, it is easier to continue what you have been doing than to quit abruptly.

As the winter continued, we continued to hear news reports from strange places. Guam. Wake Island. Manila. Bataan Peninsula. Singapore.

We heard about the Axis. Windows were blacked out. Car headlights were covered over.

Rationing began. Tires. Sugar. Gasoline. Meat.

When tires and gasoline got scarce, we knew we would not be able to continue much longer. We were driving hundreds of thousands of miles each year, burning essential gasoline and wearing out tires which might be needed in the war.

We'd been back together four years—since 1937. We had pledged not to separate again, but to stay together as a family quartet: The Blackwood Brothers Quartet.

In those years, God had been very good to us. We had progressed from a broken-down 1929 Chevrolet which wouldn't start to a new 1941 Oldsmobile.

We had moved from near starvation to the comfortable salary of forty dollars a week. We were becoming well known.

People were responding to our ministry. We were not only successful in the material realm, but in the spiritual area as well. We saw many people blessed. We saw people saved. We knew our songs were sources of comfort and encouragement.

But it was wartime. Crises come on unexpectedly. If they came when you expected them, they wouldn't be crises, would they?

We knew what was going to happen. All of us could see it coming. We knew we would have to disband for the duration of the war.

In the spring of 1942, we decided to break apart until after the war. It was not a decision which we made easily, but one which took much prayer. We still felt God wanted a Gospel music witness.

"Boys, we all know God is at work in our quartet," I told my brothers as we traveled in the early spring. "I know God has formed us together.

"But it just looks like we have no choice but to disband. I don't think it will be forever. We have got to have faith in Him. He knows what He is doing."

With that faith, we disbanded.

On our final radio show, Doyle announced. We sang

the favorite songs of the people of the Midwest.

As he closed out that final show, Doyle—and all of us—joined together in a prayer for a quick end of the war. We all prayed with everything we had that God would bring it to victorious completion and that the toll of dead and wounded would be light.

And as he ended, Doyle said: "Goodbye. God bless you all until we meet again."

We were at loose ends. We didn't know what to do. Our only income had been from singing and selling Stamps-Baxter song books.

Then a letter came from San Diego, California.

It was as if God was giving us directions through that letter.

"Dear Brothers," the letter began. It was from some good friends of ours in Iowa who had moved out to San Diego months before.

"Why don't you come out here and get jobs in the aircraft industry around here?" he asked.

R. W. and I got together and talked about going to California. Neither of us knew how long it would be before we got our draft notices.

Mim and I had no children yet and R. W. and Elaine had only a new baby, Ron. Between us we bought a car, packed our families and belongings into it, and headed out for California.

It wasn't the promised land, but we were going on faith, depending on God to keep our ministry alive and to use us for His glory.

God continued to provide. We landed jobs at Rohr Aircraft Company in Chula Vista, California, not far from San Diego. We started back to school and studied to be welders. It wasn't long before both of us passed and were certified Army and Navy Welders in the aircraft plant.

We were lonely and asked God to reunite the quartet. California was a huge mission field, and people were hungry to hear the Gospel.

Roy, Doyle, and Hilton—the rest of the quartet—were lonely too. They decided they couldn't stand having the group separated. So they came out, too.

God provided for them. They all got jobs immediately in the aircraft plant where we worked.

By His miracle, we weren't separated, but were together again and singing in California. It was almost like the early days: working days and singing when we could at night and on the weekends.

But Doyle was ill. He had been sick for some time. It was a hard blow to accept. He had been the voice of The Blackwood Brothers Quartet since we began. In Kosciusko, Jackson, and Shreveport, Doyle had been our announcer.

He was well known as our spokesman in Shenandoah.

I had been doing some of the announcing—particularly telling about our personal appearances—since Shreveport, but he was the mainstay.

His chronic stomach ailment got worse in Shenandoah and often he was unable to go to a concert. Hilton sang bass and played the piano. I announced. We started alternating the announcing on our three KMA shows.

When his health failed, I had stepped in to fill the vacuum; booking, announcing, and "fronting" the group.

"James, I am sick," he told me one morning in Chula Vista. "I can't keep up the pace of singing and working. I must go back to Mississippi."

We were sad to see Doyle leave, particularly sick, but we knew God would take care of us and of him.

Hilton stepped in for a while, and sang bass and played the piano with great versatility.

As I look back on the three years we stayed in California, I am amazed at how God provided people for us at just the right time, so we could continue to sing.

Don Smith was a former Stamps Quartet singer from Texas. He was working in an aircraft plant near ours and God led us to him. Don signed on as our bass singer.

The war years were hard on us. The strain under which we lived put our faith to a real test, just to endure the privations and struggle it was to keep together.

God had provided a way for us to earn a living in California. Welders were extremely scarce. Soon, I was asked to work part-time for a subcontractor at the Rohr plant.

Rohr was a subcontractor for Convair, makers of the Liberator Bomber.

Things got pretty hectic when I was asked to help in a friend's grocery store.

My schedule was like this: I went to the grocery store early in the morning to stock the shelves. Then I went to my part-time job where I welded four hours. I took thirty minutes for a break; then I went to my regular job and welded eight hours more.

While we were in California, we had a blessed event in our home. On July 31, 1943, James, Jr., our first son, was born.

R. W. by now had two sons, Ron and Winston.

Between family, three jobs, and personal appearances, we sandwiched in more singing.

God, it seems, wanted to keep our name alive and He continued to create circumstances in which we could become better known.

On May 10, 1944, bad news came.

"Greetings," it told R.W. "You are instructed to report for a pre-induction physical May 13, 1944."

R. W. was my nephew. But he was closer to my age than my own brothers were. Across the years, we had become closer than brothers. He was my closest friend.

The war had been going on a year and a half. The newspapers and radio broadcasts were filled with it. Casualties mounted.

Soldiers and sailors were dying around the world. The war was raging in the Pacific. Italy had been invaded. Tons of bombs were dropped on Europe daily.

"Lord, please keep R. W. safe while he is in the service," I prayed time and again as he left for induction. He was inducted into the Army on June 29, 1944.

He and I had talked about the quartet and what the future held. Both of us believed in the work we were doing.

"R.W., I will do the very best I can to keep the Blackwood Brothers going while you are gone. Then, when you get back and this awful war is over, we will work together again," I told him as he left.

We kept going the best we could, working in the aircraft plants and singing.

In late 1944, Roy and Susie decided to return to Mississippi, where they could be near Mama and Papa and Doyle. Roy had been a source of spiritual strength to us since we formed seven years earlier.

Roy had been a minister for many years before we

started the Blackwood Brothers, but had edged out of the spotlight to allow Doyle and me to mature. Roy was still our high tenor.

But he was tired and wanted to go home. R. W.'s being drafted depressed him.

Doyle was gone. R. W. was in the service. And now Roy was leaving. I was the only Blackwood brother still with the quartet. Don Smith was still with us, singing bass. Hilton had taken over R. W.'s baritone part and I was still singing lead. With Roy's departure, we were left without a high tenor, an essential part in Gospel quartets.

We prayed together before Roy left about a replacement. We found one, right where God intended: in church. Troy Chafin was stationed in San Diego with the Navy. He was from Mobile, Alabama.

The Lord led us to him in the San Diego Tabernacle, where we frequently sang. Troy joined right in with us until Roy came back from Mississippi several months later.

Roy had been gone only a few weeks before he telephoned me. He was lonesome for us, and had decided to come back to California. When he, Susie, and Cecil returned, he went back to work in the aircraft plant and sang with the quartet whenever we performed.

The Lord opened up a radio broadcast on a San Diego station. Each day at noon we sang on KGO. The Reverend George Gaines, director of the San Diego Servicemen's Center—where we often sang and where Mim had met the Lord—was instrumental in getting the program set up.

We were on KGO every day. But because we were working the way we were, we had to transcribe a week's worth of programs at one time. One day a week, we got together and made all seven programs.

It was hard, but God provided the way. He gave us the strength to go on, despite personnel changes, work schedules, and the disruption of the war.

Two other blows fell close together. They seemed devastating when they happened, but as it turned out neither was really very hurtful.

First, Hilton received his draft notice. He was very versatile and had been with us since we went to Shenandoah in 1940.

"What am I going to do, Lord," I prayed as I thought about his loss. He was our pianist. He was our baritone, singing in R. W.'s place.

As I prayed, I thought about Hilton. He was a truly big man—in height and girth as well as spirituality and talent. He was tall and weighed more than 225 pounds.

Hilton was a great pianist. He was so involved with us that if we missed a note as we sang, Hilton missed it, too.

Hilton's talent was so tremendous he could accompany nearly anybody. Even on songs he didn't know.

"Do you know such and such a song," he was often asked.

"No," Hilton admitted. "But if you'll tell me what key it's in, I'll follow you."

And he would too. He could anticipate the next chord change in a song and follow the singer without music.

Hilton had been a real show stopper in some of our concerts, because some of the pianos he was called on to play were in pretty bad shape.

We never knew what a piano—or a piano bench—was going to be like until we got to the concert site.

Sometimes Hilton would play a piano that had not been played for a long time—or at least not played as hard as Hilton played it. The ivory would start flying off the keys in every direction.

The audiences would usually break out laughing when that happened.

He was also pretty hard on piano benches. More than once an overage bench would break and Hilton would crash to the floor.

"Well," I'd say, "old Hilton will do anything to make a hit."

Just before the war, we were playing a date in Unionville, Missouri, in a little community building. I could see the dusty little building in my mind as I knelt and prayed that night in California.

I laughed as I remembered Hilton sitting down at the piano. It was as dusty as the rest of the building and it was in pretty bad shape.

Hilton started to play. Hard, like he always did.

Three or four mice came running out of the piano and scattered in every direction.

The women in the audience screamed. Some of them jumped up on chairs. Many of the men began laughing. We were guffawing.

It took about five minutes to get things settled back down and restart our concert.

As I was praying that night in 1944, all alone in California, I wondered what we were going to do. Hilton had to return to Texas for his pre-induction physical.

"Well, Lord," I prayed. "I'm just going to turn it over to You. You have been in this thing since the beginning. It is

Your quartet. When R. W. left, You kept us singing. You found a replacement for Doyle. You gave us somebody to sing tenor when Roy went home. I know You will keep us singing. I thank You for it."

On the last Sunday Hilton was with us, we were singing in San Diego Tabernacle. We finished our performance and were sad. Hilton was leaving. We had no replacement.

A fellow walked up to the front of the church. He introduced himself. He was A. T. Humphries, a Navy man from Arkansas. He'd done some quartet singing. A miracle. He was a fine baritone. Another miracle. His wife, Lavera, was an accomplished pianist.

We lost one mainstay, but God provided two. We continued to sing; with A. T. in the baritone role and Lavera playing the piano.

The second bombshell was when I got *my* induction notice.

But when the Army examined me, they decided they weren't that bad off. I was rejected.

I didn't care at the moment what the reasons were, so I didn't ask the Army doctors. I guess it was because I was so badly underweight. I also know I was working myself to death, filling the part-time welding jobs and helping my friend in the grocery store. All that, plus singing.

Anyhow, I didn't meet the Army standards, so I went back to work in the aircraft plant, where I stayed until the war was over.

Before the war was over, I heard from Hilton again. He was rejected for Army service, and offered to come back to California.

We were overjoyed, because A. T. Humphries had been transferred and we were without a baritone singer and a pianist again.

The Lord gave us chances to sing in War Bond rallies around San Diego.

We sang and promoted sales of the bonds. We were even invited to participate in a United Bond rally in Pershing Square in Los Angeles. We appeared with Roddy McDowell—who was only a boy then—and with other movie stars.

We received a citation, but the most important thing was that the Lord kept our ministry alive.

We sang wherever we could, doing the work of God.

It was difficult. Time and again I had to remind myself that the Lord is my strength. That we were His ministers—His servants.

I was tired.

Then the war in Europe was over. It ended May 7 when Germany surrendered. But we were fearful it might take another year or two of island hopping before the war with Japan was over. We were winning, but the toll was terrific.

We kept on working and singing.

Suddenly, like a wonderful stillness after the storm, peace came. Japan surrendered on August 14, 1945.

Peace. Can you imagine it? After more than three years of war, peace.

Thank God.

Chapter
9

We were going home.

First to Mississippi, and then on to Shenandoah.

I quit my job the day the war ended. I didn't wait a bit. I was ready to get back to my Father's business, full time.

I called KMA in Shenandoah. We could have our three daily programs back, beginning October 1, 1945.

I called Roy, Hilton, and Don Smith. They were ready to go back.

Roy and I started toward Ackerman. We were going to have a big family get-together before we went back to Iowa. I was anxious to see Mama and Papa.

Doyle had gotten better, but not well enough to be inducted into the Army. He had gone to Chattanooga, Tennessee where he was chief announcer on radio station WDOD. The experience he gained in announcing for the Blackwood Brothers was standing him in good stead.

He also was music director at the North Chattanooga Church of God.

We heard good news about Doyle and Lavez. She—like Mim—had been a church member when they married. But Lavez had been saved at North Chattanooga Church of God and was filled with the Spirit.

We were going to get together for a while in that September of 1945.

Late that September, we all headed toward our reappointment with God and the Midwest. We had it all figured out. Don Smith was singing bass. It had been decided Doyle would not come back to the quartet because he had a contract at WDOD.

I was still the lead singer, announcer, and booking agent.

Roy was back as our high tenor. Hilton was still filling two sets of shoes: baritone and pianist. He was going to continue singing with the quartet until R. W. came back from the Army.

God reached down and called Hilton to preach not too long after we returned to Shenandoah.

Hilton and his wife both were filled with the Holy Spirit in the Assembly of God in Shenandoah shortly after the war. After his call, we started letting him give sermonettes during our personal appearances.

Across the years since we started—whether it was Roy, Hilton, or me—we have included an appeal in our performances whenever we could. Very seldom have we omitted giving people an opportunity to come to know Jesus Christ as their Savior.

Our joy was complete when R. W. came home. It was a real Christmas present for us. Roy, Susie, and Cecil were excited. So were Mim, James, Jr., and I. Elaine and R. W.'s boys—Ron and Winston—were beside themselves.

R. W. was very important to me. I was anxious and excited when we got his letter that he would receive his discharge in December.

He arrived in Memphis on December 7, 1945, four years to the day since we had heard the terrible news on our car radio. He had been gone from us a year and a half.

God had answered our prayers and brought him back to us safely from the service. We rejoiced and thanked God for His goodness and mercy.

Elaine and the boys met R. W. at Memphis on the day of his return. After some time together, they rejoined us in Shenandoah on December 17.

God had brought us together again. On January 1, 1946, we sang on radio station KMA again as The Blackwood Brothers.

It sounded wonderful. R. W. sang in his beautiful baritone voice. Don Smith sounded the bass notes. Roy hit the high tenor sounds, and I was lead. Hilton pounded the piano in that distinctive Gospel style he had developed.

Only one person was missing. Doyle. And we were praying he would soon be a part of our family endeavor again. God answered those prayers, too, when Doyle rejoined us in a singing and management capacity later.

We were back to the three-radio-shows-a-day schedule. We were back on the road, traveling hundreds of miles a night, filling personal engagements across Iowa, Missouri, Kansas, Nebraska, South Dakota, and Minnesota.

Just after the war, staying on the road was a major miracle. Tires were rationed and the synthetic rubber tires weren't holding up too well. Sometimes we had as many as four flats in one night en route to a concert. We carried four or five spare tires.

We were always on the lookout for tires and we found Army surplus airplane tires for sale near Sioux City in a little town named Onawa.

It took some doing, but we figured out we could have the wheels on our car cut down and rewelded. It was a weird-sounding deal, but it was one of the things the Lord provided. We were back on the road.

Don Smith was dispatched to Onawa to pick up the tires. We should have known better. Don possessed the poorest sense of direction of anybody ever born.

"Don. Go to Sidney, Iowa, and turn north on Highway 275. Remember that. North. Don't forget. You turn north," I told him as he started out.

Don got to Sidney and, sure enough, turned south. Soon he and his wife began to notice the highway signs looked strange. He recounted the conversation when he finally got back to Shenandoah.

"Don," his wife said. "Are we supposed to be in Missouri?"

He scratched his head.

"No," he said.

"Well, these signs on the highway say we are in Missouri," she said.

She finally talked him into stopping at a service station. He got directions, but this time she listened in, too.

Don finally got our airplane tires.

We had the wheels cut down and re-welded. The car looked funny going down the road with those big oversize tires on it, but it was a Godsend. Without them we would not have been able to travel.

During the next four years, we traveled thousands of miles. We were back in our grind of traveling day and night. We'd drive to a concert, unpack, and perform. Then we'd pile our stuff and ourselves back in the car and start back, to be on time for our 7:30 A.M. broadcast.

It is strictly the providence of God we did not all get killed on the road. We were trapped in blizzards, ran out of gas, had blowouts, nearly got killed in car wrecks, and had hundreds of mishaps as we traveled. After each incident, we would wonder about continuing, but God always showed us He was watching over us.

One particular period of discouragement came after a bad wreck in 1946 when Hilton almost lost his life. I had to do a lot of praying about that, just to go on.

We were driving to a concert near Grand Island, Nebraska. It was dusk, a dangerous time of the day to drive. R. W. was at the wheel. Hilton was in the front seat with him. The rest of us were in the back seat.

We were just riding along, not thinking about anything much. I saw R. W. squint as the lights of an approaching car glared in his eyes.

R. W. squinted. It was hard to see, anyway, with the sun so near down.

Suddenly, right in front of us was a wagon.

I can't describe what the crash sounded like.

Roy, Don Smith, and I had time to duck down.

R. W. and Hilton were caught unprepared as the windshield of our Buick Roadmaster exploded into their faces.

The car went completely through the wagon and killed one of the horses at the front before it stopped.

Shards of glass and splinters of wood shot through the car. A plow point which had been on top of the load of hay ripped through the roof of the car, right near R. W.'s head.

One large splinter went through Hilton's neck, barely missing the jugular vein.

Hilton and R. W. were bleeding badly. Hilton was seriously hurt. R. W. had cuts on his face and hands. Roy, Don, and I were not hurt badly. But we had some little cuts on us.

Two elderly men on top of the hay wagon were thrown over the car and landed on the pavement. Neither was killed, but both were seriously injured.

Hilton was rushed to the hospital, along with the elderly men.

Glass, wood, and splinters of metal were picked out of his face. He nearly died from the effects of the wreck, but 185 shots of penicillin and six weeks later, the doctors released him from their care. He was weak, but alive.

He pulled splinters from his face for years after the accident.

The elderly men also recovered, though both were seriously crippled.

We never did understand why the wagon was out on the road without reflectors at dusk.

"Lord, is it really worth it," I wondered as Hilton was in the hospital. "Lord, should we stay out here traveling all these miles, taking all these risks driving so far?"

But, even as I wondered, I looked back across the years and remembered the miracles God had performed to keep us going. There was an assurance in my heart that we were doing what God wanted us to do. That we were to continue.

People all across the Midwest were praying for Hilton's recovery and for the safety of the quartet as we traveled.

I am thankful for our safety, but I still sorrow as I remember our most tragic accident. It occurred in 1949 as we were driving in Northwest Missouri, going to a concert.

Hilton was driving. He was moving along, trying to make it to the concert. Up ahead was a slower-moving auto. He pulled out to go around it.

The other driver speeded up just enough to block him, as he tried to pull back in.

Hilton slowed down, perplexed by the behavior of the other driver. Before he could get back in our own lane, we hit another car head on.

Our car was demolished. So was the other one. A woman in the other car was killed, just because somebody had acted childishly and wouldn't let us pass.

Our car was heavier and we were not hurt in that wreck. We were very shook up though.

There are hundreds of other instances. I am thankful God had His hand on us as we traveled millions of miles in our cars, thankful He was merciful to us and protected us from serious harm.

Chapter

10

Business was booming.

There was nearly more than we could do, with three daily radio shows and personal appearances across the Midwest.

God blessed our efforts richly after we moved back to Shenandoah in late 1945.

Now a new medium was presented to us through God's bounty. We were thinking about recording our own songs and marketing the records.

When we returned to Shenandoah, we severed our relationship with the Stamps Organization and became The Blackwood Brothers Quartet. We still handled some of their material, but we had started publishing our own song books and were selling them to help pay expenses.

"I know it'll be a lot of work," I told the quartet. "But if we are going to be all that God intends for us to be we have to look at every opportunity He presents."

We discussed the possibilities of making records. We examined costs, checked on royalties and all of the hundreds of other details which had to be worked out.

We had—right on our doorstep—the facilities for making the records. Terry Moss, who worked for KMA, had everything we needed, and he knew how to work it, too.

The time, place, and circumstances formed another of those God-arranged events in the life of The Blackwood Brothers Quartet.

The new opportunity was sandwiched in between what we already had going on. Sometimes I felt like a juggler, trying to keep all the things going at the same time.

It took a lot of work to get those records out. We did our rehearsing on the road, as we rode down the highways. We tried to find places where we could work for a little while, perfecting our performance.

When we started recording, we started arranging our own songs. Before, we had been singing straight out of the song books. Sometimes we would receive a new song book just before we went on the air for our broadcast and sing the songs cold.

"Turn to page 100," I'd tell the quartet before the engineer signaled us to start. We'd turn to the appointed page and sing a song we'd never seen before on the air.

We were pretty good sight readers and had the courage to do that sort of thing.

Things were pretty informal on KMA in the late forties. We sang songs we never sang before and played tricks on each other on the air.

We were determined to be the best Gospel singing quartet we could be, but that didn't stop us from having fun in doing it. Often, we used the same kind of inventiveness we showed in performances to play our jokes. Some of them were very elaborate tricks.

After our noon broadcast one day, we started to make the transcription for the broadcast the next morning. I got together with the engineer to pull a fast one on Bill Lyles, who had joined us as bass singer in 1947 when Don Smith returned to California.

Midway through the program, I introduced Bill and announcing our personal appearances, and advertising had a solo run, he sang a verse and a chorus.

While he was singing, I went to another studio where he couldn't see me. When Bill finished his verse and chorus, the engineer—without making any motion —turned my microphone on. He didn't let Bill know.

Bill sang and sang.

While he was sweating and singing, wondering where I was, I was in the other studio, reading cards and letters, announcing our personal appearances, and advertising our sponsor's products.

Bill sang some more. Finally, he sang all he knew and started over. He was getting frantic, looking for me.

"Folks, that's all the song there is," he finally announced. "I can't find James. I don't know where in the world he has got off to."

We had a good laugh at Bill's expense over that trick.

We were pretty informal. The good humor and tricks kept us from taking ourselves too seriously. Getting a swelled head is the last thing a performer needs. Particularly a Gospel music performer who is ministering in the name of the Lord.

We began to work more on our own arrangements, perfecting the Blackwood Sound we had started back there in 1934.

In Gospel quartets, the lead generally carries the melody. Harmony is provided by the high tenor, low bass, and baritone.

We started switching it around. We let the tenor carry the melody, or sometimes the bass. We added some high trio singing, and ended the songs a little differently than they were written.

We also experimented with inverting the parts.

There was practically no Gospel singing on records in those days. People could buy classical and popular music, along with some country and western records, but about the only Gospel records we knew of were ones recorded by Frank Stamps and the All Stars in the twenties.

When we checked out the possibilities of recording our songs, we decided to use our own label.

God was at work again, making us better known so He could spread His message of Jesus' love through us.

Those first records were big black 78 rpm discs.

"When we go into the record business, we are going to advertise our records everywhere we can," we decided just before we cut our first record.

We bought ads in every religious periodical across the country. The advertising costs hundreds of dollars, but we sold thousands of records through it.

We started carrying records to our concerts. Boxes and boxes and boxes of the heavy black discs.

In 1948, we persuaded Doyle to rejoin us.

"Doyle, have you completed your contract with WDOD?" I asked him over the telephone.

When he told me he had, I replied:

"We need you up here in Shenandoah. The mail order

business for our records and song books is getting heavier than we can handle. We need you to help us."

Well, Doyle prayed about it, and finally decided to move back to Shenandoah to be with us.

With him around, we decided to expand our base of operation even further, going into a second quartet.

We kept traveling and broadcasting, but the work got tremendous.

We didn't complain. We remembered what it had been like back in Jackson, eating nickle hamburgers and praying for a cosigner so we could buy a car.

God was blessing us. We constantly reminded ourselves we had to be faithful to Him and remember Whom we were serving. It would have been awfully easy to let the success go to our heads.

We started a second group in 1948. Roy was tenor, Doyle was lead, Johnny Dickson was baritone, and Warren Holmes was bass in The Blackwood Gospel Quartet. Johnny joined the quartet after a stint as announcer on KMA. The accompanist was Billy Guin.

The Blackwood Brothers Quartet featured me on the lead, R. W. as baritone, Cat Freeman as tenor, and Bill Lyles as bass. Hilton was our pianist.

Both groups were booked by Doyle and me, and we both traveled the Midwest.

We added the second group because we were swamped with calls for personal appearances and had to do something to keep up with the popularity we were achieving under God.

But even with the second group, the work load was so heavy that Doyle, R. W., and I had to alternate staying in the office. We interchanged the lead and baritone in the two quartets, enabling somebody to keep up with the work.

Both The Blackwood Brothers and The Blackwood Gospel Quartet were featured on the radio show, enabling us to make longer trips. We sometimes appeared on the same programs, getting into a little family competition.

We had been transcribing the early morning program, and after Doyle joined us, we went into the transcription library service.

The transcriptions were sixteen-inch vinyl discs, very flexible and unbreakable. We cut the songs and then had them pressed, just like our records were pressed.

The library records were available to radio stations, and were the things which bridged the gap between live shows and the disc jockeys.

We offered the transcriptions of Gospel songs to the radio stations across the nation. The Blackwood Brothers were pacesetters in providing this service. It was a break God provided for us, just like the wonderful breaks He gave us across the years.

Radio stations used the transcriptions a whole lot, sometimes as single cuts and other times as a whole transcribed program.

Cutting the big vinyl discs was a tricky process.

We'd often be tired and trying to get through, but recording wasn't like it is today. Now you can just change a single note if you don't like the way it sounds. Then you had to do the whole thing. There was no editing. If it was right, good. If it wasn't, you either had to do it over again or just let it go.

We had good luck. We didn't have to do very many of the programs over again.

But sometimes we did.

We were transcribing a program for a station in St. Louis. It was over except for our theme. Hilton hit a run leading into it and was ready for Don to hit the first bass note. The bass singer sang the melody and the rest of us sang on the afterbeat on our theme.

"Give the World a Smile," Don sang. It sounded awful. He'd missed the pitch.

Hilton backed up and had a shot at it again. Again Don boomed in. Again, wrong pitch. They tried it two or three times. They never made it. The whole program was ruined and we had to do it all over again.

We were the first quartet to offer a transcription service of Gospel music. Later a couple of other transcription services provided Gospel music, asking us and the Sunshine Boys to record for them.

Transcriptions were necessary in the forties, and God arranged it for us to be first in the Gospel music transcription service.

Later, when LP albums became common, transcription services disappeared, but I am thankful God made it possible for us to become known across the nation through the big vinyl discs.

Hundreds of thousands of people heard the Gospel message from The Blackwood Brothers through those records.

God was moving. We didn't know where it would wind up, but what a thrill it was to be on a ride He was directing.

Chapter

11

We were moving again.

Iowa had been good to us, but we had been in Shenandoah ten years—minus some time out for a war.

We were known across the Midwest because of our work on KMA radio.

Two years earlier, in 1948, we gained exposure on a new development: KMTV, Channel 3, out of Omaha. KMA got the license to operate the new television station, one of the first in the nation. We performed before the crude cameras of commercial television for the first time on Christmas Day of 1948.

Shenandoah and KMA had been good to us, but it was time to leave. The factors were many. First, Papa was sick. He hadn't told us about it; we found out when he came to Shenandoah for a visit.

Papa was strong and quiet. Across the years when we had been struggling and growing, Papa was our strongest supporter. When we got to KMA in Shenandoah in 1940, he and Mama got up every morning at 5:30 to listen to us sing. In the winter months, they could pick up our first live broadcast of the day at 7:30 A.M.

He had been a source of strength and encouragement to us as we sought God's will, and had been the instrument the Lord had used to instill faith into us. Now he was sick. We knew he didn't feel well. My brothers and I arranged an appointment with one of the finest doctors in Iowa for Papa.

After the examination, the doctor called us into his office.

"I have some bad news for you. Your father has some growths on his neck. We need to make some tests on them to see what they are," he told us.

Papa went into the hospital. Surgery was performed and biopsies of the lumps were sent to Iowa State University for testing. Soon the news came back: Papa had leukemia. We were stunned, even though the doctor told us Papa might live a few more years.

Papa and Mama didn't want to leave Mississippi. It was their home and they had lived there all of their lives. So we began looking south for a place to move, to be near them.

The second reason for our move was our scope of operations. We had had to keep our personal appearances confined to a radius of 250 miles around Shenandoah because of the 7:30 A.M. radio show.

We felt we had worked the territory and it needed a rest. There was a saturation point for an area. We had performed most of the places we could and now we needed to move.

Another reason behind our readiness to move on at the Lord's direction was our growing recording, mail order, and transcription service. We were outgrowing our facilities, fast.

We began to look, praying for God's guidance. Our attention was focused toward Memphis or Louisville. Both had powerful radio stations.

We opened negotiations with a station in Louisville. The contacts went on for several weeks.

But during our negotiation period, we booked a big Gospel sing in Memphis.

Oddly enough—in one of those God-inspired incidents—the All Night Sing was being promoted by radio station WMPS, one of the top stations in the area.

We went in for a promotional appearance. While we were there, we had a talk with the management of the station. They were interested in having us move there on a permanent basis.

We weren't as much interested in the money the station would pay us, but we were keenly interested in the amount of air time we would get and whether they could guarantee us a sponsor. The answers were affirmative on all counts; we struck the bargain right on the spot.

Memphis was perfect. It was about midpoint in the nation. It was a good Gospel music town. We were in the heart of a good Gospel area.

And to make it even better, we were only about 150 miles from Mama and Papa.

But every good thing has a bad side to it, too. We were excited about going to Memphis. We decided to end our association with KMA in April and start work at WMPS September first.

As we planned for the move, Hilton grew more and more concerned about it. God had called him to the ministry. He was seeking God's will for his life. It was —like most big decisions—a hard one to make.

"James," he told me one morning. "I can't go with you to Memphis. I feel the Lord is directing me to stay in Shenandoah to go into full-time ministry."

I knew such a decision was possible, but I was jolted by it none the less. Hilton had been with us ten years. He was a key man, able to play wonderful Gospel-style piano, able to sing bass when we needed it and able to perform creditably as a baritone.

We would miss Hilton, but I knew him well enough to know he was a powerful man in the Spirit. Both he and his wife were dynamic Spirit-filled Christians. We knew it had not been an easy decision, but we stood with him as he made it. We were saddened, though, because Hilton would leave a big hole in our quartet.

He agreed to stay until we left. We began to look for a pianist to work with us.

We turned to the Lord first, then we turned to our contacts.

We had a problem: we were the only Gospel quartet working in the North. We had been in Iowa so long we had lost touch with others in the South. We were out of contact. We simply did not know who was playing piano for Gospel quartets traveling the South.

I started calling people in the various groups.

"Do you know a good pianist we can get?" I asked time and again.

It was almost eerie what happened.

Time and again I got the same answer. It might have been in different words, but the response was the same: "Yeah. I know a kid. His name is Jackie Marshall. I saw him at such and such a place. I heard him play. He's really good. REALLY good."

I heard the answer often enough to start trying to track Jackie Marshall down. He had impeccable references, but he was awfully hard to find.

We finally located him. He was playing for a family group called the Spivey Family Singers in Jacksonville, Florida.

"Will you come up and play for us? We are moving to Memphis and we need you by the first of April," I told Jackie when I finally got him on the telephone.

I had never heard him play. I had never seen him. I didn't know anything about him, except that everybody I talked to had praised his playing highly.

He agreed to come to Shenandoah.

Jackie caught the train in Jacksonville, headed for Iowa. The train didn't come all the way to Shenandoah, only to a place called Hamburg.

It was about time for our noon broadcast when his train arrived so I sent Mim and Lavez over to pick him up.

They drove down to Hamburg and picked up Jackie Marshall. We were still in the studio when he got to Shenandoah.

I like to have fainted.

"What have I done?" I thought as I looked at him. The other fellows must have been standing with their mouths open, too.

Hilton was a great big fellow. He tipped the scales at more than 225 pounds.

But here was Jackie Marshall. He was about five feet, three inches tall. He had a crew cut.

He looked like he was fourteen years old.

"What have I got," I wondered. "What have I done? This little bitty fellow—"

Jackie didn't look like much.

We finally got over our shock and when he sat down at the piano that day, we didn't have any fears about how he played that instrument. He might have looked little, but he sure did play big.

Jackie joined us; we were ready to make our move to Memphis.

We regretfully left KMA April 1, leaving behind a part of ourselves, many, many wonderful friends, and many blessings from God.

There were hard times to look back on: war, fatigue, near-fatal wrecks. There were good times to remember, too: friends, seeing people saved and blessed, growing in stature ourselves, gaining fame across the nation, seeing God at work.

We spent that summer traveling across the nation, singing and vacationing. We'd sing a few days and then take a few nights off.

It was a terrific summer, the first vacation we'd had since leaving San Diego at the end of the war.

Then it was September first. Time to begin a new phase of our career.

We had packed up our belongings when we left Shenandoah early in the summer and shipped them to Memphis. Our mail-order and transcription service was booming. Roy and Doyle had to go on before us to begin the broadcasts by transcription and records while we were touring.

On that first broadcast we had a new group, but the same Blackwood Brothers Sound. Aldon Toney from Detroit was our tenor, having taken Roy's place. R. W. still sang baritone and I was still the lead. Bill Lyles carried the bass part and Jackie Marshall played our accompaniment.

We were an instant success on WMPS. Soon we had a large radio audience across the South. We were sponsored on WMPS by Milton Buhler of Buhler Mills. They made and we sold tons of Dixie Lily Flour over the Memphis station in the early 1950s.

Soon our travels broadened and it became harder for us to make regular daily broadcasts. We expanded to transcribed programs on days we were away.

When we transcribed our broadcasts, we could catch our mistakes; but on a live broadcast, when we made a blooper we just had to let it go.

Not long after we went on the air there, we were singing a song I had sung hundreds of times before on records, transcriptions, broadcasts, and performances.

Aldon, R. W., Bill, and Jackie were halfway through the song. I had the lead.

They got up to my part. I opened my mouth. Nothing came out. I had forgotten the words.

I couldn't think of the words to that song.

The quartet looked at me. The audience—and in those days we had a large studio audience—looked at me. I gawked. I searched my mind. I could remember other song lyrics. But not that one.

It went clean out of my mind. My mind was empty.

"I forgot the words. Stop and we'll start over," I told them as thousands of people listened to WMPS.

While they sang the beginning of the song, I hummed along. Still a blank. The part came nearer and nearer. I sweated. All of the eyes in the studio were on me. I knew thousands of ears were listening.

They got to my part, singing in perfect harmony. Everything was just right. Except me. I still couldn't remember.

"I still can't think of the words. Let's just forget that song and go on to something else," I told my surprised friends.

The large studio audiences which came to WMPS at noon featured a lot of people who brought sack lunches and ate while we were broadcasting.

Several years later—after a Grammy Award ceremony—I went over to congratulate the top female country vocalist of the year, Tammy Wynette.

"Tammy, I'm James Blackwood. I'd like to congratulate you on winning the Grammy this year," I told the pretty singer.

"Well, James, congratulations to you too. You don't remember me, but I remember you," Tammy told me. "When you-all used to broadcast live at noon from WMPS in Memphis, some of us girls from the telephone company there would come up every day on our lunch hour to watch you."

As we traveled and performed across the South, God used many methods to bless us and the people who heard us.

We made many friends as we sang about Jesus and the great themes of the Bible.

We were on our way again. We had started anew in Memphis. Now we were off and running for God.

Chapter

12

God was in our move to Memphis.

From the first, people accepted and welcomed us. We traveled across the South: Tennessee, Kentucky, Arkansas, Missouri, Texas, Mississippi, Alabama, Georgia.

Calls poured in. People wanted to hear The Blackwood Brothers Quartet.

Soon we were traveling more and more.

The pressures increased, but so did the blessings. Friendships developed with Gospel singing and church people throughout the whole section.

Doors began to open.

Travel began to be a problem for us. We were using large automobiles to drive the hundreds of miles.

"We've got to have more room for our records," R. W. told me as we were preparing for a trip.

He frowned as we tried to cram the public address system, boxes of 78 rpm and the newer 33-1/3 rpm "long play" records into the trunk of our car.

We decided to add a trailer for our equipment, but even then we were cramped for space.

Because of the distances we traveled, we took turns driving. Everybody but Jack Marshall was a pretty good driver.

Jackie started imagining the Highway Patrol was after him. We did drive the cars pretty fast during the early morning hours, trying to meet our tight schedule, but Jack thought the police were after him, whether they were or not.

Early one morning we were driving through Alabama and Mississippi going back to Memphis after a service on Saturday night.

Jackie was driving. The rest of us were asleep. We weren't very comfortable, but we had learned to do the best we could trying to sleep in the car. I was sitting in the front with him, slumped over.

The car rocketed through the night heading for home.

"The Highway Patrol's after me," Jack whispered. He made furtive glances at the rearview mirror. He was agitated. He drove faster.

Suddenly Jack rounded a curve and spotted a little farm house sitting off the road. He wheeled that big car and the one-wheel trailer down the little rutty dirt road that led to the house and whipped in behind the house, right in the backyard.

We woke up as the car screeched to a halt in a cloud of dust. Dogs were barking. Chickens were flying and squawking. We'd disturbed the pigs and they were squealing and grunting.

We came awake about the same time as the people in the house did.

Heads peered out the window. Children clutched onto their parents and peeked around the adults. It was a strange sight: a big black sedan loaded with men parked in back of the little farmhouse that morning.

"Jack. What are you doing?" I demanded.

Immediately the sleepy singers—now jolted into full consciousness by the events—chorused the demand.

"The highway patrol is after me," Jack explained, cautiously.

"I'm hiding."

We sat there a few minutes. We probably would have burst out laughing if it wasn't such a strange thing. Finally, we drove slowly away, when the "danger" passed.

The poor people in the house never did come out to see who we were or what we were doing. They could probably imagine a carload of thugs, complete with tommy guns and all sorts of terrible things.

We were a little leery of letting Jack drive after that, but he took his turn in rotation, since we all had to get what sleep we could.

After we were lulled back into a sense of security, Jack was driving home from Knoxville, Tennessee.

We were asleep again and the first inkling I had that anything was wrong was when I sleepily opened one eye.

All I could see was trees. We were supposed to be on the highway. But here we were, going real fast, and all I could see was those huge trees.

I almost had a heart attack.

I looked at the speedometer. It glowed dimly in the dark. We were bouncing and bumping along at fifty miles an hour through the woods.

Jack suddenly braked to a stop. He quickly shut off the lights.

I started to speak.

117

"Shh," he cautioned me. "The Highway Patrol is after me."

In a few minutes, he backed the car and trailer cautiously through the trees, following more slowly the breakneck route he had followed earlier.

I drove home.

Monotony comes as five men—even men who are close friends—travel hundreds of miles, hour after hour, day after day.

We had moved to even more transcribed broadcasts at WMPS so we could fulfill our commitments.

We picked on Jack as we traveled. He was not only afraid of the Highway Patrol, he was afraid of ghosts and spiders as well.

We worked conversations around to ghosts and spiders when we were out, trying to get Jack stirred up.

When we were out overnight, we got a large room in the hotel—a rehearsal or sample room—if they had one. That way, we could stay together and practice.

We were in Springfield, Illinois and had just finished a sing. As we headed back for the hotel, I steered the conversation around to skeletons and ghosts and spiders.

I had made some elaborate plans to kid Jack. In the afternoon, I went to a fun shop and bought a couple of gadgets: a skeleton mask and a fake spider with fur over its back. It had little springs for legs.

As we got back to the hotel, one of the boys delayed Jack in the lobby while Bill Lyles and I went to the room.

"Here, put this on," I told Bill, handing the mask to him. He put it on and started looking for a place to hide.

"I'll get behind the drapes," he said, slipping in.

Jack and the rest of the quartet came in. They had

118

continued to talk about ghosts.

"This is an old hotel," I said. "I wonder if it's haunted?"

We debated that for a while. We began to get undressed for bed. Jack walked near the drapes. A hand reached out and grabbed him.

Then Bill jumped out and stuck that skeleton mask right in Jack's face.

Jack turned white and almost fainted. We calmed him down and all had a good laugh.

The joke wasn't over, though.

When we were nearly ready to go to bed, I again mentioned that the hotel was old and probably had spiders in the room.

Everybody joined in and we started searching under the beds and behind the chairs for spiders. Jack joined in, too. But halfheartedly. He didn't want to find any spiders.

Then I started to examine my bedding. The other boys followed suit.

Jack looked over his bed, looking under the sheets and blankets.

He picked up his pillow.

I'd planted the spring-legged spider under the pillow, pushing it down so that when he picked it up, the fake spider jumped an inch or two off the bed.

Jack threw the pillow across the room. He screamed bloody murder and raced for the door. He was in his underwear, but he was so scared he didn't realize it.

He raced down the hall of that old hotel, disturbing the early morning quiet, screeching at the top of his lungs. We were afraid we would get thrown out of the hotel.

We finally caught him and dragged him back to the room.

Traveling included a lot of fun and foolishness, but it wasn't always happy.

We were in Dallas. It was 1951, and we were appearing in a revival. We'd left Doyle behind to carry on our radio program.

Things were going well. People were responding to the singing and the preaching. We saw people healed and saved. We saw families reunited. We knew God was blessing.

Midway through the revival, I got a telephone call. It was from Doyle.

Papa was ill and had been hospitalized in Memphis. Concern sounded in Doyle's voice as he told me about Papa's sudden worsening. I was needed at home.

I called the quartet together and explained it to them. We left the revival and started home.

R. W. and I flew home. It was a sad trip. We hoped we'd be in time to see Papa before he went to be with Jesus.

We gathered in Baptist Memorial Hospital in Memphis. The doctors weren't hopeful. Papa had wasted in the days of his illness.

Soon, he closed his eyes and was gone.

Floods of memories rushed across me. A sob caught in my throat. I remembered those early years. I remembered working on our sharecropper farm and living in the little houses out in the country.

I remembered picking cotton, and chopping the weeds.

But most of all I remembered his head bent down over the worn old Bible as he sounded out the words. I remembered his hands as he softly and gently held God's

Word and taught us kids what it meant to be a child of God.

"For God so loved the world that he gave his only begotten Son . . ." His words sounded in my mind as I relived for a moment those good old days of poverty, hard work, love, and faith.

" *. . . That whosoever believeth in him should not perish but have everlasting life."*

William Emmett Blackwood was seventy-four years old. He was tired and had lived beyond the span of years God promised. He'd lived a life of faith and hard work.

He was *"whosoever"* and I knew he believed.

We parted there in the cold, antiseptic-smelling hospital. But it wasn't parting. I know I'll meet him in the morning, over yonder past Jordan.

We buried the earthly remains of Papa down in Choctaw County, Mississippi, not far from our old home place, near Mount Olive Church of God.

He'd built those things with his hands.

He was going toward a mansion Jesus had built for him.

Papa had been faithful to the task God had given him; we must be faithful to the task He has given us.

We continued to sing. Whenever and wherever we could. God spread our fame and invitations continued to come in.

Soon, it became apparent we were too thinly spread.

"James, we just can't keep up this pace," R. W. told me.

I agreed.

R. W. and I discussed what we were going to do. We looked at the situation. We were getting invitations too far to drive to without being exhausted.

We simply could not continue to travel cramped in the

121

cars.

"We've traveled nearly two million miles singing about Jesus," I told R. W. as we talked about it.

"I know," he laughed, rubbing his backside. "I can feel every one of them."

We both could. We were nearly always tired and fatigued. We knew we weren't doing our best work. Some solution had to be found.

We looked up. Both to God and to the skies. The solution: an airplane.

R. W., Doyle, Roy, and I had worked in airplane plants during the war and were familiar with airplanes. After praying about it, we found an old twin Cessna. We bought it.

We hired a man to fly for us, but R. W. immediately started taking lessons so he could be our pilot.

"I've wanted to learn to fly for a long time," R. W. confided to me. "Now I've got my chance."

Soon he passed his tests and was granted a license. Bill Lyles took lessons and learned how to navigate.

Before long, we added a second aircraft: a Cessna 195. It was a smaller airplane, with a single engine and five seats.

Travel became easier as we zipped from city to city in our two airplanes.

Again God had opened the doors to an expanding ministry for us. We were off and rolling.

We were the first Gospel quartet to use an airplane to get to our concerts, and like pioneers, we had some funny experiences with the airplane.

Soon after we got the 195, we were flying south from Memphis. Bill was studying the maps and R. W. was piloting.

There was a conference up front.

"Where are we?" R. W. asked.

Bill studied the maps. He studied some more.

"I don't know. I can't figure it out," he said. "Nothing looks the same."

I hadn't been paying much attention, leaving the piloting to them.

I raised up and looked out the window: "Over yonder is Sardis Lake. Over there in the distance is Hernando, Mississippi. The next town ought to be Senatobia."

I'd traveled so many miles that I recognized the landmarks pretty well.

We had our share of close calls in the early years of flying to dates. Travel in the airplanes was so much better than driving hours and hours cramped in a car, though, that we just accepted the risk.

The Statesmen Quartet traveled with us occasionally in the airplanes. We usually flew the 195 and let them have the twin Cessna, piloted by an airline pilot friend of ours.

The Statesmen had trouble getting used to the little 195. It had a little jump seat and one person had to sit crossways. The tenor was Cat Freeman—who sang with us when we had two quartets. He was sitting on the jumpseat with his feet against the door.

Jake Hess, the lead for the Statesmen, sat in the back seat, next to the door. Cat went to sleep, and in his sleep he straightened his knees, kicking the door open.

"BOOM!!" It sounded like a shotgun. Jake nearly jumped out the door without a parachute.

On the same trip, we landed at Stephenville, Texas. After singing, our pilot friend planned to take off in the twin Cessna. We were to follow.

There were two different runways. One was 3,000 feet long and the other was only a 1,500-foot strip. The pilot got on the shorter strip by mistake.

When he got to the end of the runway, he was going too fast to stop, but not fast enough to get the altitude he needed. And, to compound the problem, there were some pine trees in the way.

He lifted it up anyway, banking sharply. He barely cleared the trees.

It frightened the Statesmen. They returned to Memphis with us, but that was their last trip aboard one of our airplanes.

Things were going very well, and our trips got longer and longer. We needed a bigger plane. We shopped around and finally found what we needed: a Beechcraft G18.

It was a twin-engine plane the Navy had used during the war. It was a real nice plane and much larger than our twin Cessna or the 195. It held ten passengers comfortably.

We had some narrow escapes it it, but we went right on flying, keeping our concert work going.

God also blessed us during our stay in Memphis when our son Billy was born in 1953.

Our quartet was busy perfecting the sound. We still had R. W. on the baritone, and I was the lead. Bill Lyles continued to sing the bass, but we had added a new tenor. Bill Shaw joined us in the fall of 1952.

We had gone through the adjustment period, and were singing better than ever. God was blessing our concerts and we were able now to sing to more people.

God stepped in and opened a new door for us in the late spring of 1954.

Arnold Shaw of Hill and Range Songs of New York City called us.

"James," he said as I answered the telephone. "Would you like to try out for the Arthur Godfrey Talent Scouts Show?"

Would I? Talent Scouts was the top-rated show on television in 1954.

That was like asking me if I would like a million dollars.

"Would I?" I shouted. "Would I? When? Where?"

I was so excited I could hardly tell the quartet about it.

The thought that we might not be accepted didn't cross our minds. We were confident we could make it.

We flew to New York in our airplane and auditioned for the show. We were accepted and told to appear the night of June 12, 1954.

Again, it was a new experience. This was national television. Television was still in its infancy, to be sure, but millions of homes across America had television sets. No other Gospel quartet had ever appeared on national television before.

We were nervous as we stood backstage, ready to go on.

"Lord, I know You're in this. Bless the people who will hear us. Use us. We want You to be glorified—" I prayed as we waited.

My hands were sweaty. We looked great: identical suits with sharp contrasting handerchiefs and ties.

Bill Shaw and Bill Lyles, Jack Marshall, R. W., and I ran on stage.

We hit the first notes of "Have You Talked To The Man Upstairs?"

When we finished, the audience burst into applause. Mr. Godfrey was obviously impressed.

When the show was at an end, he called the participants of the show back and let them do part of their number. It was plain to tell. We won.

God opened a brand new door for us; one we never dreamed about as poor boys back there in Ackerman, Mississippi, driving a 1929 Chevrolet we had to push to start.

When we got back to our hotel room that night, we thanked God for His goodness and kindness.

Mr. Godfrey had a two-hour show on CBS radio and television every weekday morning. The winner of the Talent Scouts program appeared on the shows for the next four mornings.

Audience and mail response was tremendous.

On the final morning, we sang "His Hand In Mine" and as I looked at Mr. Godfrey, he had tears in his eyes.

We flew back South and resumed our personal appearances. Tremendous crowds greeted us everywhere we went. The audiences were enthusiastic. People—more people than ever before—turned out.

We were met at airports by big crowds. We were the winners of the Godfrey television show. We were the first Gospel group ever to achieve that honor.

We were on the top.

Chapter
13

As suddenly as we reached the peak, we plunged to the depths.

We were the toast of the Gospel world. We'd won the Arthur Godfrey show; we had our own plane. "Have You Talked To The Man Upstairs?" was in the top ten sellers for RCA Victor.

We were performing as never before.

When we went on stage, people gave us standing ovations. We could hardly believe what was going on, but we were pleased over it.

We had meshed as a quartet. The notes came sharp and clear. The pitches were true. The harmony was sweet. We were singing better than we ever sang before.

Thirteen days after our last appearance on the Godfrey show, we flew into Gulfport, Mississippi, for a sing. It was a hot night, but things went exceptionally well. That night was something special. Everything clicked. There was a perfection about our performance.

People responded. People were blessed. We were blessed.

At supper—we usually eat after we perform—the quartet was by itself. The fellowship was sweet. There was a satisfaction and a feeling we had been truly used by God for something special. There was a kinship, a brotherhood.

R. W. and I were always close. He was two years younger than me. That night in 1954 I was only thirty-four, going on thirty-five. R. W. was only thirty-two.

As we ate, memories from across the years flooded in. Memories about climbing trees and catching fish in Ackerman; memories about our reunions and separations as Roy preached in some far-away place.

We thought about our start in Gospel music back in 1934. When I was fourteen and he was twelve. We were just boys.

Across the years, we had grown closer. The Blackwoods were always close, but R. W. and I had been closer than brothers, because he was nearer to my age than my own brothers were.

As we sat at the table that starry Mississippi night, it seemed that everything was just right.

From the vantage point of success, we looked back on the days in Kosciusko, when we had to farm and cut contract timber so we could buy food. We thought about Jackson, and the rooming house-hotel. We laughed at the fight we had with the fellow who worked in the hamburger stand, and how we chased him around the café when he squirted mustard on my linen suit.

"Remember how I jumped over the counter?" R. W. asked. And we laughed.

The night was perfect. After we had eaten, we all went for a walk down the beach: Bill Shaw, Bill Lyles, R. W.,

Jackie, and I making different size tracks in the sand piled up there by God.

"I don't know what's coming next, but it must be going to be spectacular. I can't believe how God has moved—I can't believe all that's happened," I told R. W.

"I'm holding my breath waiting for the next miracle to happen," I added.

We walked on down the quiet beach looking for flounder in the sand, accompanied by the sound of the surf as it rolled in from across the Gulf.

We got up early the next morning and prepared to leave Gulfport for our next concert at the Chilton County Peach Festival in Clanton, Alabama.

The weather was clear and hot—hot like it gets in the South in the summertime. There wasn't a breath of wind.

We landed at the big hangar where we were to sing. The strip was short for our twin-engine Beechcraft, so R. W. looped the plane when we reached the end of the field, bringing it to a safe stop.

It was a dirt field, like many in the South. We had used such fields time and again after we began using airplanes. We were going back to Memphis that night, but that was no problem. We had done that before, lining up cars along the runway to give us enough light to make our takeoff.

It was a lazy, relaxed sort of a day. We sang a couple of songs at noon and spent the afternoon visiting around town. People recognized us from our Arthur Godfrey show appearances. The Statesmen were going to be with us, and we enjoyed being with them.

During the afternoon, a hometown boy, Johnny Ogburn, joined us. He stayed with us, spending the time showing us around the town and introducing us to people.

Late that afternoon, R. W. suggested we go back to the airport.

"I want to take the plane up before it gets dark so I can see how much room I have for the takeoff tonight," he told us.

We accepted that, because R. W. was a careful pilot. We trusted him and his judgment with our lives.

It was about dusk when we got to the airfield. R. W., Bill Lyles, and Johnny Ogburn boarded the big blunt-nosed plane for the test hop.

I stood watching as R. W. made his takeoff checks. He started the engines one at a time and ran through the procedures. Quickly—because he had done it so many times before—he finished his pre-flight.

The stubby airplane raced down the strip and hurled itself into the air. R. W. began to circle.

It was beginning to get dark. After a while, I started to worry. They'd been up too long; I was afraid they wouldn't have light enough to land.

"I wish they'd come on back," I told Jack. "I don't like them staying up so long."

Jack didn't reply. We both stood there looking out into the gathering darkness.

Soon we heard the engines as the Beechcraft came through the evening air. The wind had freshened during the day and R. W. was going to have to land in the opposite direction.

As I looked, I could see a hill obstructing the new approach. R. W. would have to clear the hill and set it down very quickly, because the strip was so short.

R. W. came in low over the field. He had the landing

130

lights switched on and the gear was down.

I knew he was trying to get the plane down on the runway fast after clearing the hill, or he couldn't get stopped fast enough.

Quickly, I saw the gear go up and heard the power to the engines increase.

"He can't get it down and is going to have to go around again," I told Jack. "I don't like that."

R. W. circled the field and began his approach again. He was still coming in as low as he could over the hill, trying to get down onto the dirt strip. The gear was down and the landing lights were still illuminating the top of the hill.

He came in, but he had to come in too fast to clear the hill and he was still having the same problem.

"He's going too fast," I said. "He'll never get it down."

We watched as he applied all the skill he had to try to get the big plane down on the ground.

Suddenly, he cut power to drop the plane. We'd done that before, "bouncing" the airplane suddenly to the strip, hoping it would stay on the ground.

"I hope it doesn't bounce too much," I said. It did.

The big Beech was flying level and I heard the power increase again. The big motors began to whine.

The plane lifted.

"It's going straight up!" I screamed, as the ungainly airplane headed vertically upward.

"Oh, no," I prayed. "Please. No." I started forward.

The shriek of the engines was unbearable. Then the sound changed; lugged and then stalled.

Slowly, as if in slow motion, the big airplane turned over and plunged toward the air strip.

131

I began to run.

The Beechcraft struck the dirt airstrip and burst into flames.

The heat seared my face. The cabin door was open, blown off by the force of the impact. I started toward it.

"Here they are," Jack yelled.

"Perhaps they've been thrown clear," I thought as I raced toward the front of the plane.

The canopy had been shattered. I could see R. W. through the cockpit.

"He's still strapped in his seat." The thought raced through my mind.

His head was turned to the side at an unusual angle.

"Where's Bill?" I wondered, looking around.

I started into the flames, trying to reach my nephew and my friend.

But as I moved forward, somebody grabbed hold of me and lifted me off the ground.

"Let me go! Let me go! Let me go!" I yelled. "I've got to get to them!"

The fire was licking upward toward the pilot's compartment. I couldn't see R. W. any more for the smoke and flames.

I was carried away from the runway. I don't remember what happened next.

I remember the fire's being extinguished, but by then the airplane was a charred, smoldering skeleton.

R. W. was dead. Bill was dead. Their bodies were burned beyond recognition. Johnny Ogburn died with them.

I stood there on the concrete near the hangar where we were to sing. Dumbly, I watched the three covered stretchers leave the twisted wreckage.

"It can't be," my mind sluggishly thought. "It can't be. It's a dream. I'll wake up and it'll be over."

But it was true. When I came out of my dazed state, it wasn't over. It was just beginning.

After a while the people began to leave the airport. Some time later—and I don't remember how long it was—I left and went into Clanton.

As I stood there in central Alabama, telephones were ringing in Memphis.

Cecil was at the hospital, visiting his wife, Doris. They were the proud parents of their first child, Mark.

R. W. had been up to the hospital the day before—just before we flew out to Gulfport. Cecil phoned me in Clanton when he heard the news.

"We were very happy that night," Cecil recalled. "It was our first child and our first son. As we sat on the edge of the hospital bed, holding hands, the telephone rang," Cecil continued.

"Doris answered it. She was silent for a long time. I knew something was bad wrong.

" 'It can't be true,' Doris said. 'It just can't be.' "

"She hung up the telephone. 'They've been killed. Bill and R. W. There's been an airplane crash and they're both dead.'

"I thought she was wrong—that she had made a mistake. Surely not," Cecil added.

Cecil made a hurried trip to Roy's home in Memphis.

"Daddy was in the street when I got there. He was crying. Then I knew for sure something was wrong," Cecil added.

When I left the airport, my first thought was to get to a

telephone and call Memphis. By the time I called, everybody had been notified.

"Come on James," Jake Hess told me gently. "We'll take you home."

Jake put me in the Statesmen's automobile and we started out for Memphis. Although he didn't tell me then, I found out Jake was the one who pulled me back from the flames out on the runway.

I kicked bruises all over his shins and legs, trying to get away and into the flames.

We rode through the dark that night. It was dark in my heart as well as in the world. All the sunlight was gone.

As I rode, I said in my heart: "I'll never sing again. I'll never sing another note as long as I live.

"I'm through. I can never sing again."

Again and again I repeated the words in my heart.

Late that night, we arrived in Memphis. The Statesmen took me to Doyle's house, where all of the family had gathered.

Two of the Statesmen were holding me up. When they let go, I fell on my face, sobbing and crying. All of us were crying.

Elaine and Bill's wife were not there. The doctors had given them something to make them sleep.

Pastor James Hamill, our minister at Memphis First Assembly of God was there. It was he who had had to break the news to Elaine and Ruth.

As we were speeding through the night returning to Memphis, Pastor Hamill and his wife went to Bill's home.

As they knocked, Ruth greeted them with bread dough on her hands. She was surprised, but it suddenly dawned on her that this was Wednesday night and he wouldn't be standing at her front door unless something was wrong.

At Doyle's, between sobs, I told my brothers and their children what had happened.

We sat there in Doyle's house for a long time. Finally, someone took me to a bedroom. I didn't resist. They laid me on a bed and I guess I must have dozed off.

When I got up at 6 A.M. the next morning, the radio was playing a memorial to R. W. and Bill.

All of the news broadcasts had it. Walter Winchell reported it. Arthur Godfrey told his listeners what had happened. Still I couldn't believe it.

While we were waiting for the funeral, we got a word of consolation: the doctors told us the autopsies showed R. W. and Bill both had broken necks.

"They were killed instantly when the plane crashed," the doctor told us over the telephone. "They never felt the fire. They had no pain."

We were thankful for that small word of comfort.

It dawned on me R. W. probably never had time to make corrections after he tried the second landing. The Beech was set for a landing and R. W. didn't have time to make new settings. That was why the airplane went straight up into the air when R. W. applied power.

On Friday, July 2, 1954, the funeral for R. W. and Bill was held in Ellis Municipal Auditorium in Memphis. Thousands of people were there.

Pastor Hamill took part. So did Dr. R. G. Lee, pastor of Bellevue Baptist Church in Memphis and president of the Southern Baptist Convention. Jimmy Stroud, director of Memphis Union Mission and Youth for Christ, was there.

Tennessee Governor Frank Clement interrupted his

re-election campaign to fly in to speak at the service.

The Speer Family and the Statesmen sang.

I don't remember what anybody said or sang. I sat there in a state of shock. I couldn't believe it.

"God, I don't want to question You," I prayed. "But I just don't understand it. Why did they die?

"Lord, You know we're on the top. We won the Arthur Godfrey show. We have a record in the top ten. We're flying our own plane to engagements across the country.

"Everywhere people responded. We're the toast of the town. We've done something nobody else has ever done.

"I don't understand."

I never felt worse.

As I sat there in the funeral service—looking at the shining caskets—again the thoughts ran through my mind.

"I'll never sing again. I just can't. I'll never sing a note. Never again."

We'd been on the top. Now it was all finished.

Chapter
14

I was in Pastor Hamill's office after the funeral.

"I just can't go on, Pastor," I said. I was weeping. I never felt so bad or so full of despair in my life.

"I can't sing a note," I insisted. "I'm quitting—I'm giving up singing."

We began to talk. He told me of the ministry we had. He reminded me of the people who had been saved through our ministry of Gospel music.

He reminded me of what God had done. He reminded me it was God's ministry. Not mine.

"James. You can't quit," my friend said. "You can't quit even though you want to and even though you might not be able to sing as well as you have been.

"I know it might take several years to build a quartet again. But you've got to go on and do the best you can with what you have."

I didn't want to, but Bill Shaw, Jack Marshall, and I—all that remained of our quartet—climbed into my car the next day and went to Fort Worth to fulfill our engagements.

We'd been booked through July 15, when we planned

to take a vacation. We were going to honor those commitments. What we'd do then, I didn't know.

We sang the night of July 4, 1954, in Fort Worth, I guess. I don't remember. I don't know if we sang a duet or solos or what. We could have picked up a couple of people to sing with us. Doyle and Cecil went with us on some of the engagements, but I don't remember what happened that night.

Everyone tells me I sang during the next two weeks, but I don't remember singing very often. The shock just erased the memory.

Big Chief Jim Weatherington, the Statesmen's bass, sang with us sometimes during the next few weeks. Everybody was trying to help but I did what I did by rote.

People across the nation were praying for us. We got hundreds of telegrams, cards, letters, and telephone calls. People were lifting us up as we went through those hours and days. If it had not been for them I don't know what would have happened.

When July 15 came, we were free from engagements.

Some decision had to be made. Were we going to continue? Would we let The Blackwood Brothers die?

We couldn't let what God had started twenty years before die. I was nervous and under tension, but thousands of expressions of love and hope from across the nation showed me that we had to go on.

Cecil was available to replace R. W. Cecil was almost totally inexperienced. He sang baritone, but R. W. had had the most beautiful baritone voice in Gospel music. He had the greatest voice in quartet singing.

Cecil had a little group called The Song Fellows, made up of some friends of his. Jimmy Hamill, the preacher's boy, was one of the singers, and a fellow named Elvis Presley practiced with them sometimes.

First we thought Doyle would join in and sing baritone. He'd alternated on the part and filled in in 1951 when R. W. lost his voice for six months.

"James, I just can't do it," Doyle said when we talked. "I still have health problems. My stomach gives me a lot of trouble. When I travel that just aggravates it."

We knew that people would accept Doyle's filling in for R. W.

I asked Cecil to join us and he agreed. People would look favorably on R. W.'s brother joining in. Cecil also had grown up around Gospel music. He wasn't in the quartet, but he had always been around us.

I didn't want to replace Bill Lyles right away. But, as I prayed, a name kept coming back to me: J. D. Sumner.

J. D. was bass singer for The Sunshine Boys, another of the top Gospel quartets in the country.

I didn't want to make up my mind right quick. I wanted to pray more and seek the guidance of the Lord some more. I interviewed several people, talked to some more and even auditioned a couple of fellows.

I talked to some friends about the decision.

Jake Hess told me: "There is only one man who can handle your bass singing job. J. D. Sumner."

His name kept coming up. Just like Jack Marshall's had when we were looking for a replacement for Hilton Griswold back in Shenandoah.

I went home and put on a record by J. D. He had taken a secular song and changed it, putting religious words to it. I listened to it.

I called him.

God never works on one end without working on the other. He had prepared me to ask J. D. to join us. He was busy preparing J. D. to accept.

J. D. told me his story:

"I was sitting on the floor at home in Atlanta when I heard the news of the plane crash," J. D. said. "All of a sudden I had the funniest feeling. I was going to be with The Blackwood Brothers.

"I couldn't explain it. In fact, I didn't like the idea. But I had this feeling. I didn't want to go with you then. Like a flash—real fast—the idea went through my mind.

"Every bass singer in the business had applied for the job. Except me. And I didn't want it. I was happy and successful where I was," J. D. added.

J. D. was singing with The Sunshine Boys, one of the top groups.

The Blackwoods and The Sunshine Boys were very much at odds in those days and J. D. once sent word to me that he was going to whip me next time he saw me. That, of course, would have been a real brave thing for him to do, him being about seven feet tall and me about three.

We got the trouble smoothed over at a benefit, but it just shows that quartet competition was a lot fiercer than it is now.

I listened to J. D. sing that song and called him. He turned me down. I called back. He agreed to at least talk to me.

"It won't hurt if I fly down to talk to you, will it?" I asked the lanky bass.

He told me later the only reason he let me come was so he could turn The Blackwood Brothers down in person.

That weekend I called him again. He was at a sing in

Nashville: "I've prayed about it. I am convinced it is God's will. You've got to come with The Blackwood Brothers. I want you here."

He began to soften a little. He finally came to Memphis and I picked him up at the airport.

I made him an offer. I agreed to give him $14,000 a year, or pay him $10,000 plus commission, or give him part of the quartet.

"If you will give me part of the quartet, I'll come," J. D. told me. I was overjoyed.

I went to Roy and Doyle, who owned the group with me: "Brothers, I need J. D. I feel it is God's will that he be our bass singer. He will come if I give him part of the quartet. If that is the only way we can keep a good quartet, then that is the way it will have to be.

"If I am going to have a quartet, I am going to have the best quartet possible."

They agreed. J. D. became our bass singer and part-owner of the group.

I know it was God's will that J. D. join us. If I had been picking a replacement, it wouldn't have been J. D. He was nothing like Bill Lyles, either in personality, looks, or voice.

Bill had a beautiful, smooth, velvet voice. He sounded like he was singing the melody, but down in a bass range.

J. D. has a much lower voice, not nearly so smooth. They look nothing alike.

The first time I saw J. D. on stage he looked very strange to me. I went through the entire program with clenched fists. I came very close to introducing Cecil as R. W. and J. D. as Bill. I never actually did it, but I was so close that it upset me and made me even more tense. I nearly made the mistake many times in the first few months.

We had a lot of readjustments to make. R. W. had been our clown. He was always pulling some sort of high jinks on stage and getting a big laugh.

At intermission, we usually sold song books. R. W. was our "demonstrator" and got books upside down or backward. He was known for a stunt in which he walked off the edge of the stage as if he didn't know it was there. It always got a laugh.

Bill Lyles was a real quiet, reserved person in public. He was a cutup in private, but he was reserved on stage.

We knew there would be a problem of fan acceptance with J. D. He was a clown. There is one in every group, cutting up and providing comic relief during the show. He took R. W.'s place in cutting up.

He also sounded nothing like Bill. We worried that people who liked Bill's velvet smooth singing wouldn't be overly fond of J. D.'s voice. It was a drastic change for our fans.

But I was sure of my decision because I knew God was in our choice of replacements. I know it was good for us, and I am convinced it was the best for J. D. I don't believe he would have written the songs he wrote, or would have come into the prominence he has gained, without joining us.

So there we were. Reorganized. But still shattered and unsure. J. D. was our bass; Bill Shaw was the tenor; Cecil had the baritone; and I was the lead. Jack Marshall was with us as pianist.

We had some of the same personnel, but we were not the group we had been.

We'd reached the pinnacle, and plunged back. Now we had to rebuild and believe through faith that God was still using us for His glory.

Our first appearance as the reorganized Blackwood Brothers was on my birthday, August 4, 1954. It was a memorial sing for R. W. and Bill in the airport hangar at Clanton, Alabama, within sight of the still-scorched spot on the airport runway.

I did not want to go, but I knew God was impelling me to return to the spot and to begin anew.

With clenched fists and a knot in my stomach, I sang through that warm summer day. I didn't get through the trying thing by myself. God—and the prayers of thousands of friends—provided the strength I needed.

A new era in our life had started. It started in sadness and tragedy, but with God leading the way, we claimed the promise of Romans 8:28—"All things work together for good to them that love God, to them who are the called according to his purpose."

Chapter
15

We were back on the road.

We sold our other airplane and bought a seven-passenger car. We were back where we'd been; driving thousands of miles each month to personal engagements and concerts, dragging a trailer filled with records.

We were on the road days at a time, singing one night stands and traveling hundreds of miles between engagements.

When five men are in such close quarters for such long periods of time, funny things happen, which don't make much sense apart from the boredom of the road.

We were traveling with the Statesmen to a concert and were en route from Savannah, Georgia, to Charlotte, North Carolina. To relieve his boredom, Jack decided to ride with them.

Jack was ticklish. If somebody tickled his ribs, he went limp. The Statesmen got to tickling him. Jack fell onto the floor.

They tickled. Jack laughed.

Somebody got the bright idea to steal Jack's pants. They tickled him and then de-pantsed him. He couldn't defend himself. He was laughing too hard.

Somebody took his shirt off and soon he was clad only in his underwear.

They kept on tickling and he was helpless.

Soon, Jack got his chance. He turned the tables on them when they stopped at a service station for gas.

"Help," Jack screamed. "Help."

"I'm being kidnapped. Help."

Jack still looked like a little kid and he attracted a lot of attention.

The Statesmen jumped back in the car and took off again.

Jack figured in a lot of foolishness as we traveled across America.

One night in Oklahoma City, we were sitting around telling ghost stories. We had a big room and were sleeping on five roll-away beds.

Soon, it was time to go to sleep. We turned out the lights and got real still.

I got out of bed as quiet as I could and crawled up to Jack's bed. I reached in under the covers and tickled his feet.

He screamed.

"It's a spider," he yelled.

"Something's after me," he hollered, jumping out of bed to turn on the lights.

Somebody grabbed him and threw him back on his roll-away bed. It was the kind that folded in the middle and fastened at the top.

We got Jack sideways on the bed and the other four of us pulled the sides up, folding him in the middle of the bed.

He begged and pleaded, and finally we let him out.

But he was mad at us and didn't speak to us all the next day.

Jack provided a lot of comic relief for the monotony of traveling, and now we had J. D. along. Jack was still afraid of highway patrolmen, and J. D. was scared of tunnels. Between the two of them they got in some of the wierdest deals I ever heard of.

We were driving back to Memphis. We were tired; it had been a long tour.

I was ready to be home. So was everybody else.

I was driving our seven-passenger Cadillac. A mattress covered the whole back seat so three men could sleep as we drove.

J. D., Jack, Cecil, and Bill Shaw were all riding in the back.

They weren't asleep. They were just bored.

Jack started talking. "These fields sure do remind me of my days at home."

I groaned. I hoped we weren't going to have to listen to a long-winded monologue. He was a non-stop talker. He droned on and on.

Then he said a sentence which perked up my ears: "I've got the hardest head anybody ever had. I got such a hard head it's got lumps on it."

I could hardly believe what I heard.

I knew what was coming next. J. D. couldn't let something like that go unchallenged.

"I've got a pretty hard head, too," J. D. countered.

"My head is so hard I used to butt heads with an old billy goat at home," Jack replied.

"Well, I got a pretty good head on me. Anything you got

I got one better," J. D. retorted.

They bickered back and forth, each making wilder and wilder claims.

"Oh, no," I thought. It droned on and on. J. D. and Jack were always doing something like this.

"There's only one way to settle this," Jack finally said. "We have got to have a head butting contest."

"Sure thing, Jack," J. D. agreed. "As soon as we get back to Memphis."

"No," demanded Jack. "Right now!"

J. D. was pretty riled up and he didn't ever admit Jack could do something better than he did.

"What's the matter?" Jack asked when J. D. hesitated. "Are you chicken?"

Those were the magic words. J. D. was off and running.

Cecil and Bill Shaw jumped over into the front seat.

J. D. backed up as far as he could. Jack got in the opposite corner and put his head down.

The signal was given.

"WHAM!" They hit each other in the middle of the backseat. The whole car shook.

"OK, you crazy," J. D. said, backing off again.

"My word," I thought. "Surely they aren't going to do it again."

But they did.

Again and again, J. D. would back off and run his head. Then they'd crouch back in their corners waiting for the signal.

WHAM!
WHAM!
WHAM!

I got a headache just watching them. I finally had to

slow down real slow because I almost had a wreck watching them butt heads.

"I'm dying," J. D. finally admitted after about the thirtieth head butt.

Jack chortled and claimed himself the winner. He had the hardest head. He was right. J. D.'s head hurt for a week.

"That was the stupidest thing I ever did," J. D. admitted. "I may still have a brain concussion for all I know. But, boy, we had a head butting contest!"

When we traveled, we ate wherever we could, whenever we could.

We ate some pretty good food, but there were some terrible exceptions, like the time in New Mexico when we stopped at a little place to eat.

"I'll have a grilled cheese sandwich," I told the waitress.

"Yes, sir. Would you like that hot or cold?" She answered.

I figured I was in the wrong place, so I ordered a bowl of cereal. It's hard to mess up a bowl of corn flakes.

But, the main event of travel was J. D. and Jack.

We were all married but Jack, and it came Jack's turn to go to the altar.

Jack was very nervous, but he asked J. D. to take part in the wedding anyway.

J. D. and Cecil were the candle-lighters.

It was a very solemn occasion and Jack had spent a lot of money on his wedding. It had to be just right.

Candles were all over the front of the church.

J. D. and Cecil started walking slowly toward the front, carrying the gleaming brass candle lighters.

They were supposed to keep pace with each other and light the candles on each side at the same rate.

Cecil got ahead of J. D.

J. D. started watching Cecil. Cecil edged further out front lighting his candles faster.

J. D. hurried but was still behind. He edged the wick out of the candle lighter a little. The fire blazed up. He pushed a little harder.

Suddenly about a foot of wick came out of the candle lighter. J. D. kept on trying to light the candles, but it was like trying to ignite them with a piece of burning rope.

Whoosh!

The whole wick went up in smoky flame.

J. D. started swinging the candle-lighter around. He waved it all over the front of the church. People ducked and put their hands up.

Everybody on his side of the church looked like they wanted to run.

J. D. claimed it was an accident, but Jack always thought he did it on purpose just to mess up the wedding.

Chapter
16

I woke up sitting on the edge of my bed.

I was sweating. My heart pounded in my chest.

"R. W. and Bill really weren't killed. They're OK," I said to myself.

Gradually I came fully awake. It was a dream. Ever since the crash, it kept coming back. The circumstances would change a little bit, but the dream was always the same.

I was in a concert hall singing. R. W. and Bill walked in the back of the hall. They'd just been away somewhere. They hadn't really been killed.

The dream depressed me.

All of the old questions started to flood my mind: "Why? When we were the toast of the Gospel world? Why? When we had done something no other Gospel group had ever done before? Why? When it looked like we were at the peak?"

The dream haunted me. No matter whether I was at home in my own bed or away, I would awake suddenly filled with a hope that R. W. and Bill were still alive.

I knew they weren't alive. I'd seen them die.

I sat there on the edge of my bed. I couldn't keep on like this.

"God," I prayed. "You've got to give me peace about this. Please take these horrible dreams away. Please, I ask You, take these terrible questions out of my heart. I love You. I know the accident was part of Your plan and purpose. I don't understand it. But I believe it. Help me accept it."

As I prayed, I knew that God had answered my prayer. I knew He was still God—the God who had performed so many miracles in my life and in our ministry.

I do not remember exactly when the answer came, but that answer is etched sharply in my mind. It came in the form of a dream—a dream brought to me by the Holy Spirit.

I was in Heaven. It was a beautiful place, but my eyes were centered on Papa, who'd gone to be with Jesus in 1951.

R. W. was just getting to Heaven. Papa was very close to R. W., and regarded him more as a son than as a grandson.

Papa spotted R. W. R. W. spotted Papa.

They looked at one another. Suddenly R. W. rushed toward Papa. Papa held his arms out wide. They hugged each other, shouting and crying.

I awoke from the dream, weeping. But the tears I cried were not tears of despair and depression. They were tears of joy. I had seen the reunion of two of the people I loved.

My tears were of peace. God ministered to me. Never again did I dream the terrible dreams which troubled me after the tragedy.

We started to rebuild from that point on. We were not the group we had been, but, under God, we were going to be the best we could.

We worked and perfected our talents, singing and working toward being the very best there was.

Everywhere we went, people accepted us. Everywhere we went, people told us of the power of our witness.

We were going to continue. We were going to sing. In spite of what had happened, we were going to have faith.

People across the nation told us our witness helped them face tragedies and difficult places.

God demonstrated his mercy and his goodness to us in the summer of 1956.

"Why don't you come up and be on the Talent Scouts Show again?" Mr. Godfrey's representative asked me over the phone.

"You are not the same group you were, and we'll give you a new place on the show. You don't even have to try out. We'll just book you for September."

We were overjoyed. We were different. But God was the same.

Again, we went to New York. Bill Shaw, Cecil, J. D., Jack, and I sang on national television.

Our excitement was high. God answered our prayers and when the results were in, we were hands-down winner.

We got to spend another week on Mr. Godfrey's daytime television and radio show.

I know God was telling me I was right in not giving up, even though I would have in despair. He was showing me He honors and blesses our faith and determination.

We were going upward again.

God was moving strongly as we expanded our horizons

even further, determined to take the Gospel to every place we could.

As I look back, I am amazed at how God has always had a person, a word, or a method for us, just when we needed Him most.

He had a cosigner for our car note back there in Jackson. He provided Mr. Stamps and Stamps organization support in the low times of the late thirties.

God provided a place to work and the strength to keep going in the horrible years of World War II.

Just as He opened the doors to the 1954 and 1956 wins on the Arthur Godfrey show, he had a person ready to fill a place when we needed help.

Don Smith, Troy Chaffin, A. T. Humphries, and Lavera. Jack Marshall. Hilton Griswold. J. D. Sumner. Bill Shaw. Cecil. John Hall. Ken Turner. Dave Weston. Tommy Fairchild. Larry Davis. Pat Hoffmaster.

Just the right person at just the right time.

He's provided for us, reproving, ministering, and using.

Sometimes across the years, I've been a little careless about emphasizing the spiritual part of our ministry. We can get pretty tired when we have a long tour of one night stands. It's an awful temptation to let our singing become just a show—mechanical.

But the Lord always sits me down and shakes me.

"Don't forget the essential message, James," He tells me.

It's easy to get in a rut. But every night God makes me see it is a different audience.

"For some people out there this may be the only opportunity they'll have. You'll never sing to some of them again, James. This may be the last time anybody will get to witness to somebody here.

"Treat each night as if it is important. Treat each song and each concert as if it is crucial. It is to somebody," the Spirit speaks to me.

We want to make it count. God has made so many things count in my life. I want to make my life count for Him.

Chapter
17

"Let's buy a bus," J. D. said.

We all looked at him.

"A bus?" I said.

We were riding down the highway in our 1954 Cadillac seven-passenger sedan.

"Just think how much more rested we would be for the concerts. The more we rest, the better we sing," he argued. "The better we sing, the more the Lord can use us to reach people."

It was a new idea. No other Gospel quartet—nor any other performing group—used a bus. Everybody was using big cars, like ours.

"Maybe we ought to get us a train," snickered Cecil. "We could each have a special car. Then when we wanted to go places we could use it."

Bill Shaw chimed in. "Yeah. Another thing we need is a steamboat. When we get a concert in St. Louis or New Orleans, we could just get on our steamboat and ride down the Mississippi."

We all thought up some reason why a bus wouldn't work.

I gave it some serious thought. I weighed whether it would be practical. I thought about how much it would cost and how long it would take us to travel on a bus.

J. D. kept on that spring of 1955, pushing his idea.

"I've been looking at those buses like they use at the airports to shuttle people around. I think something like that would be good for us," he argued.

He came at it from every angle he could think of, finally admitting he had been thinking about a bus ever since he started with the Sunshine Boys years ago.

Soon, he wooed some of the members of the quartet to his idea.

He kept on talking. Soon he advanced the key argument:

"James. I can put the quartet in a bus for very little more money than you have in this 1954 Cadillac."

I replied: "You can't."

"Yes, I can," he argued.

"Okay, J. D. If you can do it, then we'll get a bus," I agreed.

We were en route back to Memphis when I agreed to the deal.

The next morning, bright and early, Cecil and J. D. headed down to the Continental Trailways Garage. They had their eyes on a 1947-model Arrowcoach.

"James," Cecil said as soon as I answered the phone, "we have a bus for you to look at. Come on down and see what you think."

I went down and looked the bus over. I okayed the deal and we bought the bus. The Cadillac was put on the market.

Immediately, J. D. began fixing the bus up. First, he

had it painted. It was a glistening white, with huge letters spelling out our name along the side: "**Blackwood Bros.**"

The outside looked spectacular, and we had obtained the bus for only a couple of hundred dollars more than we got for the Cadillac.

"What are we going to do about the inside?" I asked as we studied the stripped-out interior.

We thought about it and planned it. We had no models to go by because we were the first quartet to use such a vehicle.

Finally, we hit on an idea.

"Let's put lounge seats in so we can all rest," I suggested. Then we'll all have room to stretch out so we can sleep."

We got the Arrowcoach on the road.

The other groups thought we had lost our minds.

"You're crazy. That'll never work," said a member of the Statesmen when we pulled in for our first engagement. "You'll be back in a car before long."

Jake Hess chimed in. "Aw, a bus isn't practical at all."

The Statesmen were traveling with us most of the time. Soon, some of the members of the quartet started riding with us. Before long all of them had spent some time aboard our vehicle.

The last holdout was Hovie Lister, the Statesmen's manager. Finally, he rode with us. Hovie decided it was a pretty good idea. The Statesmen became the second Gospel quartet to join us on the bus route across the nation.

In the first three months we had the bus, repairs cost us more than $3,300.

"J. D., this has got to stop," I told him after shelling out a big repair bill. "You take the responsibility of over-seeing the bus."

From there things changed. J. D. knew I was about to drop the whole idea. I was beginning to think the whole thing wouldn't work. That it cost too much money. But I kept my mouth shut and was willing to give it a fair try.

J. D. soon came up to me in the studio after we had transcribed our broadcast for radio station WMPS.

"We don't have a driver anymore," he announced.

"What are we going to do now? How are we going to travel?" I asked as hundreds of questions whirled through my mind. We didn't have a car. We had some dates coming up. Now we didn't have a bus driver, either.

J. D. saw how perplexed I was.

"I'm going to drive," he announced casually.

"Can you drive?" I asked. I would have as easily believed he was going to fly by flapping his arms.

"Well, I drove a truck for years," he said. "I don't see why I can't drive a bus."

Bill Shaw squalled. "I ain't riding with you. You aren't going to kill me."

Everybody gave J. D. a rough time over it, but he was bound and determined to prove a bus would work out for a Gospel quartet.

J. D. drove the bus, and taught everybody else how to wheel it around, but primarily depended on help from Cecil to spell him on long hauls.

Learning to drive a bus that big was hard for some of us to do. Cecil learned by driving down any four lane high-way we came to, just steering. When any gear-changing had to be done, he yelled for J. D., who rode in the seat right behind him.

I determined it was my turn. I had waited for a while, watching and getting my courage up. Finally, I told J. D. I wanted to drive.

I got in the seat.

J. D. began to laugh. He slapped his leg and laughed and laughed.

"You're the funniest looking thing I ever saw. A little bitty fellow in a great big bus," J. D. howled. "You can barely reach the steering wheel."

Soon J. D. quit laughing and started frowning.

"I have to take care of this bus. I'm responsible for it," he yelled as I ground the gears. "Double clutch it. Get the motor going the same speed," J. D. said, grimacing as I ground them again.

I kept trying, but I missed the gears.

J. D. did a pretty good job the next six months we were on the road. We had been out a lot in repairs in the first three months we had the Arrowcoach. He kept the repairs down to eighteen dollars in the six months he took care of the bus.

I finally learned how to drive the bus, but small as I am, I still must have looked funny sitting up there in the driver's seat of that big old bus.

One night, after I got the hang of driving better, we were coming in from Chicago. The brakes were pretty funny on that old bus and it was the wintertime. The brakes, when they got wet, didn't work very well.

We were coming in on the Interstate, and the toll booth was getting closer and closer.

I pushed the brake pedal. Nothing. I shoved it harder. We kept cruising along at fifty miles an hour.

I just steered it through the toll booth to the surprise of

the toll takers.

The quartet thought it was funny and started waving as we roared through the toll booth. They laughed as I finally got the bus to stop. I trotted back a half mile to pay the toll.

We had some problems with that first bus. Problems with vehicles always seem to happen in the middle of the night in the middle of nowhere.

We were in Texas, headed outbound from Houston. Everything was closed down and the roads were deserted.

The bus began to vibrate. We ignored it for a while, but it got worse. Then the generator quit working.

J. D. got out to investigate. He, Cecil, and Ronnie Blackwood—R. W. 's oldest son—checked everything they could think of.

"I found the trouble," J. D. told us. "The universal joint bolts broke, and caused the vibration. It vibrated the generator clean off the motor."

The rest of us went back to bed and J. D. and Ronnie caught a ride to the nearest town.

When they returned, all three of them got under the bus. Ronnie was the only one small enough to get up in where the work needed to be done. J. D. and Cecil were both full-grown men and Ronnie was only fourteen when he was with us.

Cecil handed Ronnie the parts. J. D. held the flashlight and told him what to do. It was a messy job. Ronnie got covered with grease and oil.

Cecil got out and started wiping himself off as the last bolts were being tightened. J. D. eased out from under the Arrowcoach.

Finally, Ronnie rolled out. He looked like a greaseball. He was covered with grease and oil.

J. D. started to laugh.

Ronnie took offense. He reached into the grease pan and got a big handful of gooey, black grease.

He reached out, calm as you please, and, starting at J. D.'s head, wiped it clear down over his face, even filling his mouth with goo.

Like a shot, Ronnie was off and running down the road. J. D. yelled and took off after him.

The rest of us had gone back to sleep but the commotion woke us up. J. D. returned to the bus, covered with grease and listening to the laughter of the rest of us. He never did catch Ronnie.

J. D. kept the job of driving the bus for us, but it began to be a burden.

We had been on a concert tour and were headed home from Knoxville. J. D. was tired. We all were. He started and got as far as Chattanooga in the mountains.

He had gone as far as he could go. He woke Cecil.

"Get up, Cecil," he said. "I need some help. I'm so sleepy I can't keep my eyes open. I need some rest."

Cecil was so tired he couldn't move.

"J. D.," he said without even opening his eyes. "I'll give you twenty dollars to drive for me."

Nothing doing, boy," J. D. mumbled. "I wouldn't do it for forty dollars." Cecil groaned: "Well, if you won't do it for forty dollars, why don't we put my twenty dollars and your forty dollars together and hire us a driver?"

The next morning, J. D. approached me: "Me and Cecil are going to hire a driver."

He said he could get a driver for fifty dollars a week, so I gave him an okay to go ahead. I was getting pretty tired of driving, too.

They scouted around and a few days later J. D. walked into our hotel in Nashville.

"Well, I hired a driver," he announced.

"Who is he," I asked, looking around.

He pointed at Bundy Brewster.

I was as shocked as I had been when I saw Jack Marshall back there in Shenandoah.

Bundy looked like a little kid, maybe fifteen. He looked like a big overgrown baby. He was six feet, five inches tall and weighed 300 pounds.

Bundy told J. D. he was an expert bus driver. Not only that, he added, but he could fix buses too.

He said he was twenty-one.

We found out he hadn't told us the exact truth. First, he was only nineteen. Second, he couldn't drive a bus. Third, he couldn't fix one, either.

J. D. was proud of his "find" and bragged to Hovie Lister and other members of the Statesmen about our new bus driver.

The next day, with our new driver sitting behind the wheel, we started off in the Arrowcoach for a date in Tupelo, Mississippi.

Bundy got us started, but we lurched and jerked.

"He's just nervous," J. D. assured me. "He'll settle down in a little bit."

It got worse. Bundy kept running off the road and grinding the gears.

"My word, what have I hired?" I wondered, glancing at Bundy and J. D.

We got to Tupelo, but not too well. We were scheduled

to sing in a building on the fair grounds. Out front was a little canopy that wasn't attached to the building, but covered an entrance.

When we drove through the gate, the Statesmen were all standing around watching us.

Bundy headed for the canopy.

"Surely he's going to stop. No way he's going to hit the canopy," J. D. murmured. We were all watching, horrified.

Bundy did. He just drove straight into the canopy.

The Statesmen broke up. They just laughed and laughed. They rolled on the ground.

We got off the bus. J. D. wouldn't get off. He was humiliated.

"Come on, J. D., you've got to get off," I said.

As he did, the Statesmen all greeted him with catcalls and embarrassing questions.

"Hey, J. D.," yelled Jake Hess. "You got a bus driver? Where did you get him?"

Hovey Lister remarked about our "fantastic driver."

Bundy—and J. D.—never lived down the Tupelo canopy.

Bundy's driving improved after that, but he was still terrible on starts and stops. Sometimes he would throw us out of bed lurching off or slamming to a stop.

Finally, J. D. had all of it he could stand. He took a glass of water and sat it on the dash: "Okay, Bundy. You spill a drop of that and you're fired."

That explanation helped Bundy's driving a whole lot, though a few days later, a car suddenly pulled out in front of the bus. Bundy slammed on the brakes, spilling the water. It wasn't his fault, but he carried on something

165

terrible about spilling the water.

Bundy worked for us for twelve years, but while he learned to drive, he didn't learn to sing a lick.

The "Singing Bus Driver" became a fixture in our concerts. It was sacrilegious to let him sing Gospel music, so we let him butcher "You Are My Sunshine."

He couldn't carry a tune in a bucket, but it was comical to listen to him "sing" the song. He recorded it and sold a lot of records. Louisiana Governor Jimmie Davis, who wrote the song, even bought a copy of it. He probably couldn't believe it, either.

Our first bus was an odddity, not only to our fellow Gospel singers, but to the public as well. That first summer, we offered guided tours through it and thousands of people toured our white Gospel bus.

After more than a year with our old Arrowcoach, we decided it was time to get a new bus. We decided to get a diesel bus this time, to save on fuel costs since we were traveling 100,000 miles a year.

J. D. and Cecil found a used bus and picked it up in Dallas.

Once again we were in the refurbishing business. The first job was to get it painted. J. D. showed me a color sample and I approved it.

When we got the bus back from the painters, J. D. drove it out to show it to me. I was shocked.

"That's not the color we picked out," I said.

J. D. was as sick as I was.

The bus was purple.

The one bright spot about "Old Purple" was answering questions people asked about the color.

"Who picked out that color?" people asked. I was always glad to tell them: "It wasn't me."

The bus was a jinx. Peculiar things were always happening to it. It caused us more trouble than any vehicle we ever had.

It really cost us money. One month we spent $10,000 on repairs, including three engine pullouts.

The old purple bus caused us many headaches, and we had so much trouble with it, we had to pray a lot to keep from losing our tempers.

Old Purple got us in some unusual predicaments, but the weirdest was when we were on a tour in the East. We'd finished a concert in Charlotte and were headed for Harrisburg for a sing the next night. We drove all night.

The next morning around daylight, we were in the hills near Raleigh. Bundy was driving. We were all asleep in our bunks.

Bundy topped a hill, and as he started down the other side, the drive shaft fell out. The spinning part hit the air diaphragm on the bus, knocking out the brakes.

The bus hurtled down the hill, with Bundy steering and shouting.

"Help," he hollered. "J. D. James. Cecil. Anybody. HELP!"

The bus plunged down the hill and up the other side.

It didn't have quite enough momentum to make it to the top of the next hill, so it gradually coasted to a stop. But it was on an incline, and it started rolling backward picking up speed.

Bundy was still screaming.

J. D. woke up. He dashed up to the front. "Stop the bus," he yelled.

"I can't," Bundy yelled back.

"What do you mean, you can't?" J. D. demanded.

By this time all of us were awake.

"I don't have any brakes," Bundy explained as calmly as a man rolling backwards downhill could.

"Well," J. D. demanded. "Put it in gear."

"I can't," Bundy said. "I don't have any gears. The driveshaft fell out."

J. D. jumped up to the front and between the two of them they kept the bus on the concrete as it rocked back and forth four or five times before stopping in the middle of the valley.

Luckily there was no traffic.

J. D. got dressed and caught a ride to town, where he made arrangements for a wrecker and a new bus.

The Harvesters Quartet from Charlotte still had our old Arrowcoach, although they had a new bus.

Bill Hefner, their manager, okayed our proposition to use the old bus, but we had to promise to be responsible for it.

"We'll be totally responsible for it," J. D. promised as he hung up.

The old Arrowcoach and a driver got to us about 10 A.M. We off-loaded our records, PA system, and gear from "Old Purple" and headed out toward Harrisburg.

Bundy was going to join us when Old Purple was fixed.

We were glad to be on our way. But it was a hot day and we'd been out on the road about an hour when the Arrowcoach's motor overheated and stopped. The engine froze up.

There we were again, stalled in the middle of nowhere. It cost $750 to get the old bus repaired.

We caught a ride to a little store and started calling

around. We found the nearest car rental place was in Petersburg, Virginia.

"Fine, we'll still have time to get to Harrisburg if we hurry," I told the quartet.

We found two men in the little town who agreed to take us to Petersburg, where two cars were waiting on us.

One man agreed to take our gear and three of us to Petersburg for twenty-five dollars.

J. D. talked to the other man. He wanted to keep the cost of the ride to less than twenty-five dollars.

J. D. told the man we needed a ride to Petersburg.

The man hemmed and hawed. He finally told J. D. he'd transport them for five dollars each.

J. D. wasn't listening.

"I'll give you twenty-five dollars and not a penny more," he exclaimed.

No sooner had he said the words than he realized what he had done.

J. D. really heard it from the rest of us about his "good deal," and "saving" us fifteen dollars.

The men took us back to the broken-down Arrowcoach. We loaded the cars with records and took off for Petersburg. But just before we got there, one of the cars had a flat. The man didn't have a jack so we had to find one.

It was getting later and later.

Finally, we got to the car rental agency, loaded our gear, and took off for Harrisburg.

Before we got through Baltimore, the tread started coming off a tire on one of the rental cars. It was 10 P.M. before we got that changed and left Baltimore. We still had ninety miles to go.

We made a hurried call to the Couriers, a Gospel singing group promoting the Harrisburg sing.

We finally pulled in at 11 P.M.—late but not shut out. We went on stage and sang an hour.

After our performance, we went to a hotel for a little sleep. At 3 A.M., Bundy pulled in "Old Purple." We piled aboard for a trip to Chillicothe, Ohio, where we were to sing the next afternoon.

We were all exhausted. All of us took thirty minute turns at the wheel.

We arrived at the auditorium in Chillicothe at 2:30 P.M., just in time to get unpacked and sing.

That had to be the longest thirty-six hours we ever spent.

"Old Purple" finally got so bad we had to get rid of it.

The Statesmen and The Blackwood Brothers went together and bought two new diesel buses. For the first time, we had a brand-new bus.

That bus lasted seven years and we never missed a date during the whole time.

For the past several years, we have driven larger, customized buses, completely appointed with bunks and lounge chairs.

Our new bus has a color television and complete sound system.

God again has provided a method for us to travel. As we cross the country singing and serving Him, He has provided the way.

Chapter
18

"You are not going to dictate the terms to the Lord, James. He dictates the terms to you."

Pastor Hamill was talking to me in his office at First Assembly of God in Memphis.

"You'll never receive the infilling of the Holy Spirit until you quit telling the Lord what you are not going to do."

The words sank in.

I had been seeking the infilling—or baptism—of the Holy Spirit for years. The harder I sought, the more it eluded me.

Often I wept in frustration at my inability to receive the blessing God had for me.

I knew it was real. I had read over and over again the passages in the Book of Acts about the baptism of the Holy Spirit.

Acts 2:1-21, when the Holy Spirit had come with a sound of a mighty rushing wind to the disciples as they waited in the Upper Room.

Acts 8:4-17, when Philip preached the revival in Samaria and Peter and John went there to lay hands on the new converts.

Acts 9:11, when Saul became Paul and was saved and filled with the Holy Ghost.

Acts 10:34-36, when Cornelius received the Holy Spirit, and began to speak in tongues just like the disciples did on the Day of Pentecost.

Acts 11:15-18, when Peter defended laying hands on a gentile and told the other disciples how Cornelius had been filled with God's wonderful Spirit.

Acts 19:1-6, when Paul laid hands on the Ephesian followers, and they were filled with the Holy Spirit and wonderfully began to worship God in languages they did not know.

I had worn my Bible out at other places: 1 Corinthians 12, 13, and 14, and Luke 3:16, when Jesus promised to baptize His followers with the Holy Ghost and fire.

I had never wanted anything so bad as I wanted the infilling of the Holy Spirit.

For years—beginning when I knelt at that old altar at Mount Olive Church of God in Ackerman as a boy of six years old—I had wanted all the blessings of God.

I knew what the Bible had to say about it, based on the words of Jesus and Paul.

I knew other blessings awaited the born-again believer in Jesus Christ. I was born again and I wanted the power to live the Christian life the way my Savior wanted me to.

My prayer life was good. I read my Bible every day. God was blessing our concerts. People were saved. People were healed. People were truly touched by the power of God.

But something was missing.

I wanted the power Jesus promised in Acts 1:8—"*But*

ye shall receive power after that the Holy Ghost is come upon you."

That's what I was doing in my pastor's study that morning in 1967.

During that summer, I was seeking the baptism of the Holy Spirit more than ever.

I ran over in my mind those I had seen receive this wonderful blessing of God. Hilton Griswold—Jack Marshall—Mim—my own sons, Jimmy and Billy.

"I know it's important to my Christian life," I told Pastor Hamill. "I know God wants to give me this blessing. But, the harder I seek, the harder it is—"

I told my pastor what I had been saying all along.

"The one thing I want to be sure of is that when I receive the infilling of the Holy Spirit, it is all of the Lord and none of me," I said.

I reeled off a list of reasons. As we had ministered across the country, I had seen many people I felt were doing it all themselves.

"I see a lot of charismatics doing it all in the flesh. It is more of them than it is the Lord," I said. "I see a lot of fanatical things that I can't believe are from the Lord.

"I am afraid I'll do that myself," I said.

My pastor agreed. "I know how you feel, James. I know what you mean.

"But you'll never receive what God has for you as long as you hinder Him. And your attitude is a hindrance. You are so busy telling Him what you won't do that you are not listening to Him tell you what to do."

That stunned me. I had been so sure that I wanted the Lord to do *all* of it, and now here was Pastor Hamill telling me I had to get rid of even that attitude.

173

"God wants you to take the first step. In receiving the infilling, you have to be willing to open your mouth and begin to speak. The Holy Spirit will give you the utterance—He will speak the words through you.

"But you have to step out first and open your mouth," my pastor added.

"You have to be willing to say, 'Lord, I'll do anything You want me to do.' Instead, you are saying, 'Lord, I want it to be all of You and none of me.'

"You pray earnestly to receive, then just wait passively for God to baptize you in His Spirit.

"That's wrong. You have to ask, then open your mouth and begin to speak, trusting Him to take over from there.

"He will honor your faith."

I knew Pastor Hamill was right. God had honored our faith time and again—like when we continued to sing after the crash. Like when we went to Shenandoah. Like when we began our ministry back there in 1934.

"Do you remember the story of Peter walking on the water?" Pastor Hamill asked.

I was perplexed. What did the story of Peter have to do with the infilling of the Holy Spirit?

"Yes, I do," I replied.

"Who performed the actual miracle of walking on the water?" he continued.

"Jesus did," I answered.

"Did Peter have anything to do with it?"

"No." I replied.

"You are absolutely right. Peter did have absolutely nothing to do with the miracle."

He paused.

Then, he continued: "But Peter did do something.

Didn't he?"

I was surprised: "He stepped out of the boat."

"That's right," Pastor Hamill added. "What would have happened if Peter had never stepped out of the boat?"

"Nothing," I replied.

"That's what is happening to you. You have got to step out of the boat. You have got to take the first step of faith. If you step out—just like Peter did—God will take over and perform the miracle.

"You are just sitting and waiting for Him to do something TO you. He wants to do something WITH you," he added.

Our conversation continued, but I had a lot to think about. I wanted it to be all of the Lord and none of me, but that very attitude had hindered me from receiving the blessing God intended for me.

I still wanted all God had, but I didn't want to do it in my own power under the guise of the real thing.

I was forty-eight years old and had been in Gospel music thirty-three years.

We left on a tour that day.

The personnel of the quartet had changed. Big John Hall was singing bass in place of J.D. Sumner, who had moved over to head the Stamps Quartet.

John and I had talked many times as we traveled about my desire to receive the baptism of the Holy Spirit. He was one of the most spiritual men who ever traveled with our quartet. His quiet strength was a source of power to us all.

I knew John was praying for me.

God was orchestrating our tour, preparing for my infilling.

One of the early stops of that tour was at Evangel Temple in Kansas City.

I told Pastor G.W. Hardcastle of my conversation with Pastor Hamill, and told him I was still seeking the infilling of the Holy Spirit.

As we left en route to Indianapolis and our next stop, he handed me a slim paperback book.

"James, I think I have just the book you need. Read it. It'll give you further help," he said.

When we settled down on the bus, I looked at the book. It was *They Speak With Other Tongues*, by John Sherrill.

I sat in the front section of the bus and began to read. Excitement began to build. By the time I got to page 17, I ran to the back of the bus.

I slipped into my sleeping compartment and pulled the sliding doors shut.

I began to praise God.

"Thank You Jesus. Oh, I love You Jesus—thank You. Praise Your Holy Name—how wonderful You are—"

Soon the sound of my praises changed. I was praising God in a beautiful new language—a language I'd not learned—a language I'd never heard before.

Tears ran down my face. I never felt such joy in my life. My heart swelled. There was a lump in my throat. God's presence filled my soul.

It seemed like the whole compartment glowed.

I ran to John's compartment.

"John," I shouted. "I've received the infilling of the Holy Spirit."

He threw back the sliding door.

"Praise God!" he yelled.

Soon, everyone on the bus was awake. We shouted and

176

praised and sang for hours.

God is so wonderful.

I had grown up around pentecostals. I knew the experience was real and for today. But God didn't force it down my throat. He wooed and cared and loved. Finally, with gentleness and tenderness, He filled me with His precious Holy Spirit.

Soon, I was asked to give my testimony at our church in Memphis. It was the weekend after the Gospel Quartet Convention, and there were 2,000 people there, a lot of them friends of ours from all over the country.

Our work is interdenominational, and is supported by people from nearly every church. Many have no knowledge about the baptism of the Holy Spirit.

I told what God had done for me, tracing back to the old altar in Ackerman. And coming up to the joyous night in the back of the bus speeding to Indianapolis.

"Just think. There are so many people who don't realize there is anything for them beyond just being born again—I thank God there is more—so much more—"

I told them that "surely everybody who really loves the Lord will have an open mind and an open heart—

"Surely you want everything God has for you."

When the invitation was given, a close friend of ours, London Parris, came forward to go to the prayer room.

Later, the Lord brought London to sing bass for the Blackwood Brothers, but that night, he had an appointment with God in the prayer room at First Assembly of God in Memphis. London was filled with the Spirit that night.

I thank God for the boldness He has given me since that night on the bus. I thank Him for the wisdom.

But most of all, I thank Him for the strengthened relationship I have with Him. For the peace—for the abiding faith—for the sweetness it is to talk to Him now—for the communion and fellowship I have with Him.

Thank God for His wonderful mercy and kindness!

Chapter
19

It's dark in the auditorium.

The people have all gone. Those who lined up for prayer have been met personally and we've prayed together.

All of our equipment has been loaded on the bus. Loud speakers, microphones, records, books, and the personal items we carry.

It was a good concert. The power of God filled the auditorium. I'm thankful for it.

I want to take a look before I, too, climb on the bus for a trip to our next stop.

Where the people have been is dark. But as I look, the memories of a lifetime flood in.

God has been good to us. His grace and bounty have covered us like a shield. He has taken care of us in the good and the bad. He has kept us going when nothing but His strength would do.

He has spread our name around the globe: Scandanavia, the Holy Land, Europe, Alaska, Hawaii, all across the whole United States.

We've been given exposure on national television.

He's used radio, television, personal appearances, records, and hundreds of other methods to make us well known.

It's been a long way from the tiny town of Ackerman in the red clay belt of Mississippi back in the poverty-stricken days of the Great Depression.

I can hear the sobs as I look out into my memory.

I can hear the laughter of the good times.

We've had a lot of fun as we have traveled and sung.

Sometimes people mistake getting religion with getting a long face. Meeting Jesus is not like going to the undertaker, or getting the news that your mother-in-law is coming to spend the winter.

When I received Christ it was a joyful, happy experience. My burden of sin was lifted and rolled away. I had God's promise that my sins were cast into the deepest sea to be remembered no more.

My name is written in the Lamb's Book of Life. Hallelujah. I've got something to shout about.

Sometimes I get emotional during our concerts. Well, I've got something to be excited about. I saw a man throw a fifty-dollar Stetson away during a football game. What excites me is not the football game, but the thrill of meeting and knowing Jesus Christ and living for Him and seeing what He can do in the lives and hearts of people.

So often when we sing, people begin to praise God and clap their hands. Occasionally you can spot people in the audience who don't know what to do.

I usually tell them: "You may say, 'We don't act like this in our church.' But we ain't in your church tonight. Somebody has probably already spotted you here tonight and they're going to talk about you anyhow, so you may as well come on and join us and have a good time."

Lots of people act like they belong to the First Church of Refrigeration, but I believe in what the Bible says: "Let the redeemed of the Lord say so." I believe in praising the Lord.

As we travel and praise and sing, God has piled on blessings faster than we can count.

We've won five Grammy Awards for the top Gospel album.

The Dove awards keep coming to me as the top male Gospel singer.

The quartet keeps winning award after award.

We've been on national television a number of times.

Our calendar is full of concert dates.

I am thankful both of my sons—Jimmy and Billy—have picked Gospel music as their life's work. Billy played with the group for a while and now is with another group.

Jimmy, our "champion bus driver," is doing more and more of the lead singing, assuming a larger part of our work.

Cecil is doing much of the management of The Blackwood Brothers now, relieving me of some duties.

Roy went to be with the Lord in 1970 and Doyle in 1974, leaving me as the only member of the original group.

I am thankful God has raised up a new generation to continue the work Roy, Doyle, R. W., and I started so long ago.

God is still blessing as we sing about His Son.

Again and again people stop us as we are at concerts to tell us about what we have meant to them.

Salvation—deliverance—a burden lifted—a spiritual

need met—

On and on it goes as God uses.

Not long ago we were singing in an auditorium in Greenville, South Carolina. We were singing "I'll Meet You In The Morning." I jumped down into the audience and began to shake hands with the people there.

As I was standing there, an elderly lady moved slowly up the aisle, aided by a walking cane. She finally got to me and put her arms around my neck.

Tears were streaming down her face.

I knew the message of hope of Jesus.

God has taken us to the Holy Land, and we have sung where Jesus walked. We sang in the Moslem cemetery at the site of Calvary.

You'll never know the thrill it was to stand there on that morning, watching the sun come up, singing "The Old Rugged Cross" at the place where Jesus died.

Or the thrill of singing at the mouth of the open tomb, where he rose again.

As I looked out over the dark auditorium, my heart was filled with Jesus' love.

"Thank You, Lord," I prayed. "Thank You for all of the good times and all of the bad times. Thank You for Your faithfulness, even when we weren't faithful.

"Thank You, Lord, for using us.

"Thank You for what has gone before. Thank You for the blessings and miracles You are fixing to do. Thank You for what is coming."

"Thank You Jesus!"

Then I walked from the dark auditorium and headed for our bus. It was humming and ready. The quartet was aboard. The equipment was loaded.

"Okay," I said. "Let's go."

WHEREVER PAPERBACKS ARE SOLD
OR USE THIS COUPON

504 LAUREL DRIVE
MONROEVILLE, PA 15146

·SEND INSPIRATIONAL BOOKS
LISTED BELOW

Title   Price   ☐ Send
                                                       Complete
                                                       Catalog

_____   _____

_____   _____

_____   _____

_____   _____

_____   _____

_____   _____

_____   _____

_____   _____

Name   _____

Street _____

City _____ State _____ Zip _____

Suggested Inspirational Paperback Books

FACE UP WITH A MIRACLE
by Don Basham $1.25

This is a fascinating book about God the Holy Spirit bringing a new dimension into the lives of twentieth-century Christians. It is filled with experiences that testify to a God of miracles being unleashed in our lives right now.

BAPTISM IN THE HOLY SPIRIT: COMMAND OR OPTION?
by Bob Campbell $1.25

A teaching summary on the Holy Spirit, covering the three kinds of baptisms, the various workings of the Holy Spirit, the question of tongues and how to know when you have received the baptism of the Spirit.

A SCRIPTURAL OUTLINE OF THE BAPTISM
IN THE HOLY SPIRIT by George and Harriet Gillies   60c

Here is a very brief and simple outline of the baptism in the Holy Spirit, with numerous references under each point. This handy little booklet is a good reference for any question you might have concerning this subject.

A HANDBOOK ON HOLY SPIRIT BAPTISM
by Don Basham $1.25

Questions and answers on the baptism in the Holy Spirit and speaking in tongues. The book is in great demand, and answers many important questions from within the contemporary Christian Church.

HE SPOKE, AND I WAS STRENGTHENED
by Dick Mills $1.25

An easy-to-read devotional of 52 prophetic scripturally-based messages directed to the businessman, the perfectionist, the bereaved, the lonely, the ambitious, and many more.

187

SEVEN TIMES AROUND
by Bob and Ruth McKee $1.25

A Christian growth story of a family who receives the baptism in the Holy Spirit and then applies this new experience to solve the family's distressing, but frequently humorous problems.

LET GO!
by Fenelon 95c

Jesus promised a life full of joy and peace. Why then are so many Christians struggling to attain the qualities that Christ said belonged to the child of God? Fenelon speaks firmly—but lovingly—to those whose lives have been an uphill battle. Don't miss this one.

VISIONS BEYOND THE VEIL
by H. A. Baker $1.25

Beggar children who heard the Gospel at a rescue mission in China received a powerful visitation of the Holy Spirit, during which they saw visions of heaven and Christ which cannot be explained away. A new revised edition.

DEAR DAD, THIS IS TO ANNOUNCE MY DEATH
by Ric Kast $1.25

The story of how rock music, drugs, and alcohol lead a youth to commit suicide. While Ric waits out the last moments of life, Jesus Christ rescues him from death and gives him a new life.

GATEWAY TO POWER
by Wesley Smith $1.25

From the boredom of day after day routine and lonely nights of meaningless activity, Wes Smith was caught up into a life of miracles. Dramatic healings, remarkable financial assistance, and exciting escapes from dangerous situations have become part of his life.

SIGI AND I
by Gwen Schmidt $1.25

The intriguing narrative of how two women smuggled Bibles and supplies to Christians behind the Iron Curtain. An impressive account of their simple faith in following the Holy Spirit.

SPIRITUAL POWER
by Don Basham $1.25

Over 100 received new spiritual power after hearing the author give this important message. The book deals with such topics as the baptism as a second experience, the primary evidence of the baptism, and tongues and the "Chronic Seeker."

THE LAST CHAPTER
by A. W. Rasmussen $1.45

An absorbing narrative based on the author's own experience in the charismatic renewal around the world. He presents many fresh insights on fasting, Church discipline, and Christ's Second Coming.

A HANDBOOK ON TONGUES, INTERPRETATION
AND PROPHECY by Don Basham $1.25

The second of Don Basham's Handbook series. Again set up in the convenient question and answer format, the book addresses itself to further questions on the Holy Spirit, especially the vocal gifts.